Intimacy Craving Jesus

A Guide from Beginnings of Intimacy to Full Intimacy with the Lord

Kevin Lesh

Intimacy with King Jesus: A Guide from Beginnings of Intimacy to Full Intimacy with the Lord
Copyright © 2023 by Kevin Lesh

All rights reserved. This book or parts thereof may not be reproduced in any form, stored in a retrieval system, or transmitted in any form by any means electronic, mechanical, photocopy, recording, or otherwise without prior written permission of the publisher, except as provided by United States of America copyright law.

Cover art: Jean Keaton
Cover design: MadeForMore.io
Collaborator and Editor: Jill M. Smith

Unless otherwise noted, Scripture quotations are taken from the King James Version (KJV) of the Holy Bible. Public Domain.

Other Scripture quotations have been taken from the following translations: Amplified Bible (AMP), Amplified Bible Classic Edition (AMPC), Brenton Septuagint (Brenton), Christian Standard Bible (CSB), Good News Translation (GNT), International Children's Bible (ICB), Modern English Version (MEV), New American Standard Bible (NASB; NASB95), New Century Version (NCV), New English Translation (NET), New International Version (NIV), New King James Version (NKJV), New Living Translation (NLT), The Living Bible (TLB), The Passion Translation (TPT), The Voice (VOICE), and Young's Literal Translation (YLT). Full copyright information is found at the end of this book.

All emphases in Scripture quotations (boldface) and other quotes are added by the author; italics added are indicated.

Author contact: Kevin Lesh
www.cravingjesus.tv

Cataloging-in-Publication Data is on file with the Library of Congress

Paperback ISBN: 9798392227136

10 9 8 7 6 5 4 3 2 1
1st edition, April 2023
Printed in the United States of America

Dedication

To Jesus: I owe You everything. Thank You for being mine.

To Mom and Dad: Thank you for showing me Jesus all those years ago. I am eternally grateful.

To my daughters, Havana and Berlin: You are beautiful and lovely! I pray Jesus captivates your hearts as He has mine.

When You See Him as Lover

Some might say,
"Why wait for Him like this?
I already have Him."

Because, when He walks in,
His demeanor is so lovely.
His face is so bright.
His eyes are like fire,
Beautiful to the sight.

His breath is sweet.
His voice is so precious.
His words are like dynamite.
They explode in your vessels.

He calls you by name.
He calls you His own.
He whispers to you,
"Come away. Let's be alone."

It's these moments when He makes you His.
He makes you His bride.
He exposes His heart
For you to see inside.

It's not words on a page,
But a Person in the flesh.
No longer just stories,
But now you feel His breath.

Because when you see Him as King,
He makes you known as rightful heir.

When you see Him as Lover,
He sweeps you off your feet.

When you meet Him as Victor,
He hands you the keys.
There's only one King, one Lover, one Victor.
He is all of these.

By Kevin Lesh

Contents

Dedication... iii

Poem When You See Him as Lover iv

Preface... ix

Introduction.. xiii

Chapter 1 Getting to Know Him...1
         The Importance of Saying Yes to Intimacy with God

Chapter 2 Spending Time Alone with Him 37
         Practicing His Presence

Chapter 3 Experiencing His Presence..............................59
         Understanding Who and Where He Is

Chapter 4 Placing Your Confidence in Jesus....................87
         Knowing He Is with You

Chapter 5 Flourishing with Him 115
         Setting Your Focus on Jesus

Chapter 6 Meeting Jesus in Different Ways 147
         Experiencing the Power of His Names

Chapter 7 Experiencing Jesus in Worship 169
         Worship as a Way of Life

Chapter 8 Enjoying Your Time with Him 215
         A Look at Intimacy from the Song of Solomon

Chapter 9 Experience His Power in Personal Ways 255
    Multiple Ways to Practice His Presence

Chapter 10 Coming Away with Jesus 289
    The Importance of Spending Time Alone with Him

Additional Copyrights 296

Don't just survive your life. Thrive! 301

Preface

I grew up in church. Regular attendance was a way of life for my family and me, and we were there pretty much all the time. But during all my experiences, from children's church through youth group, I never remember experiencing the presence of Jesus. He was a picture on a coloring page. He looked down at me from a painting on the wall. He was the subject of my Sunday School songs. But that was as real as it got—if you would even call that "real." It wasn't until I was in my thirties that I had what I would describe as a face-to-face experience with Him. To say that my life was changed would be too much of an understatement.

I was thirty-three years old and was at the end of myself. I had spent all my adult years up to that point building my kingdom. I had married, had kids (two daughters), and had even served thirteen years in the United States Navy, with four ship deployments and a tour in Afghanistan.

After years of "building" but going nowhere, I felt so empty, lonely even. I had started visiting a church for the first time in more than fifteen years. Tapping into my former teenaged self, I found myself sitting in the very back—the highest spot—of a church that could seat around two thousand people.

When others stood for the worship songs, I sat. I just sat and had a heart-to-heart with God. I started telling him "Thank You" for the things in my life—my childhood, my time in the Navy, my wife, and my two awesome daughters. I knew exactly where I was going with this heart-to-heart, and so did He. When I reached the point where I asked God to please take care of my wife and daughters when I "go," and then I said goodbye, something broke inside me. And that's when He showed up. In all His splendor!

That indescribable moment when He met me at the highest point of that church auditorium . . . the best way I can explain it is that He showed off. Psalm 145:5 says, "They speak of the glorious splendor of your majesty" (NIV). But how can someone truly describe that "glorious splendor." I know I can't. The beauty and love He showed me, the beauty and love that He is, created a moment and an experience that I will remember for eternity.

From that encounter onward, I became fully captivated by Him. I began to crave Him like an addict would crave his next fix. That craving for Him and His word drove me into a closet—a literal closet—just so I could be alone with Him. Nothing else mattered, and nothing else was enough. My heart had been stolen; my eyesight had been taken over by His beauty. Eyes open or closed, I literally saw Him everywhere.

Fast forward four years, and I was working for both a church and a Bible college. My rocky marriage and my family had been restored. And I had completed the first draft of this book. Life was good, and I was even more enamored by this wonderful Lover and Savior, Jesus Christ.

And then the rug got pulled out from under me. The newly restored marriage crumbled. And I found myself living in a separate house from my family, working a new job, no longer working for my church and Bible college, and now sharing custody of my daughters with their mother.

As the draft of this book grew digital cobwebs, and I was reintroduced to a life of singleness and a too-quiet townhouse, I was forced to confront my own beliefs and teachings about intimacy with Jesus. Was His promise that "I will never leave thee, nor forsake thee" (Heb. 13:5) just words on a page? Or was that promise written for me? One thing I am happy to say is that I never doubted this promise. Never questioned Him. He had fully captured my heart. Even when things were at their worst, I felt like Peter when Jesus asked His disciples, "Do you want to leave?" And Peter said, "Where would I go? Who would I go to? Only You have the words of life" (John 6:67–68, paraphrased).

Looking back now, I can see why God led me to learn, experience, and then teach intimacy with Him. It wasn't only to help others. But it was to help me, too. In my desire to help others know Him, He was preparing me for this very moment in my life. His promise to never leave was most certainly written for me. And as

He and I have continued to build on the foundation of intimacy, our relationship has grown deeper, more intimate—even more than I had ever thought possible.

What I have found through my time seeking Him, in both the distant and the recent past, is that He has always been the One seeking me. He has always been the One diligently going after me. The biggest evidence of His pursuit of me came in the way of four little words:

"Just sit with Me."

Jesus

Although it was obvious what "sit with Me" meant, at the time, I had no idea what it would or should look like. I began to take blocks of time out of my day—starting as small as two minutes—and just "sat" with Him. The intimacy that I have experienced and continue to experience through those times means that the draft of this book can no longer stay buried and gather cobwebs. Others must hear how much He loves them. How much He loves you! He earnestly desires to be with you. He longs for you. Will you sit with Him too? Come with me, and let's sit with Him together.

Introduction

When you think of the word intimacy, what do you think of? Do you think of a close friendship? Do you think of an even closer relationship? Does the thought make you blush?

When you think of intimacy with Jesus, what do you think of?

I've done a lot of street and church ministry. Along the way, I have met some longtime believers who have made comments about how I talk about the Lord. Instead of only using names and phrases like the one I just used ("the Lord"), I also call Him names like my Beloved or my Lover, or I call Him Beautiful or Lovely. I talk about Holy Spirit (no the) as a person, One who is closer to me than my very breath.

These longtime believers tell me—sometimes with tears—that the way I talk affects them, that they have never experienced this level of closeness. Their pastors or teachers have taught topical, "practical" things, or they have been expository teachers, teaching the Bible book-by-book or verse-by-verse. But these people have never been taught how to have an intimate relationship with their Savior. Of course, I'm not saying that book-by-book or verse-by-verse teachings are useless. I'm just saying that many believers only get this type of teaching. Maybe their leaders have deep, personal relationships with God, but they haven't taught their people how to have their own.

Or maybe they don't know that intimacy with Jesus can actually be taught and learned.

If any of this describes you and your experience, then you have come to the right place. The teaching and practical applications in this book can launch you forward into the amazing relationship God desires to have with you. Holy Spirit will lead you into the freedom and bliss that is intended for you, His bride!

Keep in mind, though, that intimacy takes time. Just like any intimate relationship does. In this book, we will practice His presence; we will practice sitting with Him. But we will start small. As we learn more about intimacy and build our "sitting" muscles, we will go deeper with Him. And then the "we" part will disappear, and the focus will be just on you and Him.

I believe Jesus has put this book into your hands. As you read it, it is my prayer that you will experience the manifest presence of Holy Spirit. You will encounter Him anew—or you will experience Him, perhaps, for the first time.

The Practicing Intimacy Approach

Throughout this book, you will see a scriptural framework that may not follow a traditional Bible study. In Bible study groups or during church sermons, the leader or pastor will usually teach from one main translation. Sometimes a teacher will explain the Greek or Hebrew behind a specific word, or sometimes he or she may offer a phrase from a different translation. But always, the teaching is directed back to that main translation.

In personal Bible study, I think this one-main-translation format gives too much voice to one person or group of people (such as the committee of a certain translation). I study the Bible by reading it in different versions and translations. This technique allows Holy Spirit to be my Teacher. He becomes the Speaker in my ear and my heart. John 14:26—in several translations—calls Him "the Helper," One who has been sent to "teach" us. First John 2:27 explains that He is our main Teacher and the only One we really need. So, while biblical teachings are beneficial to the body of Christ, and I listen to certain Bible teachers myself, my desire is for the Lord to be the main voice in my life.

I want this for you as well, which is why I have included multiple translations in this book. Sometimes you will see the same verse in several translations on the page, while other times, I may give a suggestion of additional translations to read for certain verses. You can find these various translations in online databases, through computer or phone apps, through Bible software, or by old-school means—actual hardcopy Bibles in multiple translations. By the way, when you see a verse with no translation mentioned, this will always be from the King James Version of the Bible (with the exception of chapter 8). I love both the beauty and the challenge of reading the KJV.

In addition to the different versions of Scripture you will find, you will also see what I call an **Intimacy Activation Prayer** at the end of each chapter (or sometimes in the middle). I think of these prayers as a way of praying off the wrong thoughts and praying on the right ones. Through Jesus, God has given us everything we need, so our lack of experiencing this "everything" is almost always an awareness issue. We need to know that He has given us everything. The activation prayers give us the opportunity to speak out what we've learned, declare our righteousness, and exercise boldness and confidence in Him. This speaking out greatly helps our thoughts and our environments to line up with what He says.

As I said before, intimacy takes time. It is also purposeful. When God told me, "Just sit with Me," I didn't accidentally end up in His presence. I had to on-purpose take time out of my day, get to a place where I could be alone and get over my awkwardness of feeling like I could be talking to the air. I, as a man, also had to get over the strangeness of falling in love with a Person who is seen as male.

I want to urge you to be purposeful in meeting with him. So this book will lead you to **Practice His Presence**. These are times when you will set this book aside, set your Bible study tools aside, and just start talking to Him. One thing I do encourage you to have with you when you spend time in His presence is a journal of some sort. You can use any kind of notebook that you like, or you may want to use the prayer journal that accompanies this book, which has chapter-specific devotionals, additional activation prayers, and plenty of pages and spaces for you to record what the Lord speaks to you. Because He will speak. He promises that "the Spirit of truth . . . will guide you into all the truth; for He will not speak on His own, but whatever He hears, He will speak; and He will disclose to you what is to come" (John 16:13, NASB).

I have found that practicing intimacy with King Jesus has been the key to survival and success for me. Being in His presence and being intimate with Him is a way of life for me. I'm excited to walk you through this process so that you, too, can experience your own intimate relationship with your Savior.

Our First Practice

Before we leave this introduction, let's have our first practice. Set a timer for two minutes, close your eyes, and talk to him. The prayer below is what I prayed out loud when I led a group of students into a two-minute practice. I call it speaking "sweet nothings" to Him. Skim it or skip it. This is your time with Him. Not mine.

Set your timer. And go!

Lord, I love You so much. I love You so much, Lord. I thank You that You are King. I thank You that You are King of my heart. You have stolen my sight. You're the only thing I want to look at. Thank You, Lord. I thank You that I'm singularly looking at You. I thank You that You've captivated me—fully captivated me with Your mind and Your power and Your splendor. Thank You, Lord. You're so beautiful. I praise Your name, Lord, the most beautiful. Thank You, Jesus. I thank You that You're the Comforter. It's Your delight to sit with me, to converse with me. I thank You that it's not a job or a task to You… You love it. Thank You, Lord. All honor and glory are Yours, Lord. All the honor and the glory are Yours. There's none like You; there never will be. Thank You, Jesus. I worship Your name. I worship Your name, Lord. Thank You, Jesus, the most majestic. All majesty is Yours. None compares to You; none compares to You, Jesus. Thank You, Jesus. I thank You that You're the victory. My victory is in You. I don't have to hold the victory. It's all on You. It can't be taken from me because my King holds the keys. Thank You, Lord. The King holds the keys.

Wow! That was a quick two minutes.

Chapter 1

Getting to Know Him

The Importance of Saying Yes to Intimacy with God

*I have asked one thing from the L*ORD*; **it is what I desire**: to dwell in the house of the Lord all the days of my life, **gazing on the beauty of the L**ORD and seeking him in his temple. For he will conceal me in his shelter in the day of adversity; he will hide me under the cover of his tent; he will set me high on a rock.*

Psalm 27:4–5 CSB

We must, we must, we must get alone with God. Spending time in His presence is the most important thing a Christian can do. The most important place a Christian can be. Practicing His presence could be labeled as a "Christian discipline." But to me, that sounds like an obligation when it's actually the most joy a person could ever experience.

You can probably see that I am passionate about this subject—which is more than simply a subject. For me, it is life itself. And I believe it can be that way for you too.

Most of you reading this have had or will experience a romantic relationship at some point in your life. Even if you have not experienced this type of relationship, you have most likely seen one portrayed in a movie, on TV, or in a book. Regardless of the way a relationship starts or even ends, all "good" ones have one thing in common—the couple's overwhelming desire to spend time together. They can't get enough of each other. Notice, too, that it's also between two people. They may spend time in public, but if you've ever seen newlyweds or even newly-datings, you probably noticed that they only have eyes for each other.

So what is the secret to their desire? Well, if you back up to a real or hypothetical example of a first date—or worse, a blind date—and remember the awkwardness, the stretches of silence, the halting small talk. Perhaps this first date evolved into something more; perhaps it went the way of so many others. But what made that *first* encounter so uncomfortable?

You didn't know each other. Not only that, but you may have questioned if the other person even wanted to be with you in the first place.

Since this life and our experiences here are all we have to go on, at least before we are born again, it is expected that we compare everything else to those experiences. It's no wonder so many Christians—from baby to longtime Christians—get uncomfortable about the idea of spending long stretches of time alone with Jesus: *What would we talk about? What if it gets awkward? Does He even like me?*

We'll talk about those first two questions in the next chapter. That third one? Let's talk about that one right now because it's probably *the most* important.

I mentioned this before, but I want to say it again: if you are not experiencing all that God the Father has for you, all that Jesus died to give you, all that Holy Spirit is working out inside you, it is an awareness problem—a problem that can be solved! What I mean is that the problem is not with God. The problem is that we don't know who we are in relationship with and what we have now because of that relationship.

Second Peter 1:3 says that "His divine power has given to us all things that pertain to life and godliness, *through the knowledge of Him*" (NKJV, italics mine). Notice that His power has already given "all things" to us, but it's "through the knowledge of Him" that we experience those things. We experience His goodness and everything we need by knowing Him.

A Relationship Starts . . .

If we think again about that first-date question, the answer can be summed up with John 3:16: "For God so loved the world, that he gave his only begotten Son, that whosoever believeth in him should not perish, but have everlasting life."

It's easy to skim over that verse without really reading it. I purposely used the King James Version for that reason. It may be the first (or only) verse you ever memorized, and it was probably in the King James when you did. But let's look at it in different versions, and then we'll talk about what's really packed into this seemingly simple verse.

> For this is how God loved the world: He gave his one and only Son, so that everyone who believes in him **will not perish but have eternal life**. (NLT)
>
> For this is the way God loved the world: He gave his one and only Son, so that everyone who believes in him will **not perish but have eternal life**. (NET)
>
> God loved the world so much that he gave his one and only Son so that whoever believes in him **may not be lost, but have eternal life**. (NCV)

First, notice the parts of this verse that I did not put in bold. Notice how much God loves you. He gave His only Son to you—the greatest gift imaginable. He gave us the very best. And it was a gift that could never be given back. It was a total commitment to *you* from the very first date—or "from the foundation of the world" (Rev. 13:8).

This sounds like *He likes you a lot.*

But the mystery goes deeper than that. God Himself became a Man, He left heaven, He came to earth, and He gave Himself over to an excruciating death, so you wouldn't have to see death yourself. Of course, this doesn't mean that your body won't die. We live in a mortal body; the apostle Paul calls it a "tent" and says that our bodies will be gone someday (2 Cor. 5:1, various translations).

What the Father did was give you, me, the entire world, the opportunity to believe in Him through the Son so that we won't perish, or as the NCV puts it, so "we may not be lost." This believing in Him means that we will live forever with Him. But because this is a book about intimacy with Jesus, this might be a good place to say, "But wait, there's more!"

If we aren't intimate with the Lord, the idea of living forever with Him may not seem as exciting as it really is. So, let's focus on that final phrase. The King James Version says, "everlasting life," but almost every other English translation calls it "eternal life." Our life experiences, past teachings, and understanding of our own language may cause us to shrug, thinking we know what eternal life means.

Of course, Jesus explains it best. During His last night on earth, Jesus prays the most intimate of prayers to His Father. He asks the Father to glorify Him, and then He says, "You gave the Son power over all people so that the Son could give eternal life to all those you gave him" (John 17:2 NCV).

He clearly states that He—Jesus—has the authority to give us eternal life. (And we already know that if He has the power to give, He *will give!*) Then He defines what this gift actually is in John 17:3:

> And **this is eternal life**, that they may **know You**, the only true God, and Jesus Christ whom You have sent. (NASB)
>
> And **this is eternal life**: that people **know you**, the only true God, and that they know Jesus Christ, the One you sent. (NCV)
>
> Now, **this is eternal life**—that they **know you**, the only true God, and Jesus Christ, whom you sent. (NET)

This verse explains this gift of eternal life as something like a math equation: "Eternal life = knowing Him."

So eternal life doesn't just mean meeting Jesus after death, living in heaven, or spending eternity with God. It is all that, but it's also more than that. It's now. It is knowing Jesus right now as a Brother, Friend, Savior, Father, King, Master. It's knowing every facet of His being. It's being intimate with Him.

Get to Know Him

What does the word "know" mean? The English word know is used hundreds of times throughout the Bible, over two hundred times in the New Testament alone. But I want to focus on seven passages where the specific Greek word (*ginōskō*) is translated as "know" and link it to John 17:3 above.

When an angel appeared to Mary to announce that she would become pregnant with God's Son, she didn't understand how this could physically happen:

> Then said Mary unto the angel, How shall this be, **seeing I know not a man?**
>
> Luke 1:34

The New Living Translation makes it clear what Mary was asking: "But how can this happen? I am a virgin." Her virginity lasted through her pregnancy and the birth of Jesus. Matthew 1:25 says,

> And [Joseph] **knew her not** till she had brought forth her firstborn son: and he called his name JESUS.
>
> But he did not have sexual relations with her until her son was born. And Joseph named him JESUS. (NLT)
>
> But he did not have intimate relations with her until she gave birth to the son. And Joseph named the son Jesus. (ICB)

From these passages, it is clear that the word "know" means to be intimate—very intimate. In these cases, "knowing" is used as a euphemism for sex (a euphemism that goes back to the very first humans, when Adam "knew" his wife in Genesis 4:1). Yet, Holy Spirit chose to use this word throughout the New Testament to describe the nature of His close relationship to us.

Let's look at the use of this word in John 10:14–15:

> I am the good shepherd, and **know** my sheep, and am **known** of mine. As the Father **knoweth** me, even so, **know** I the Father: and I lay down my life for the sheep.
>
> I am the good shepherd. I **know** my own, and my own **know** me—just as the Father **knows** me and I **know** the Father—and I lay down my life for the sheep. (NET)

Again, the word "know" means intimately close. Jesus is the Good Shepherd; He knows His sheep (that's us). The New English Translation uses the phrase "my own." This indicates a type of oneness, much like the oneness married people experience together. This is not knowing God from a distance like His people did in the Old Testament. It is deep, personal, and intimate. And this "knowing" goes both ways. Jesus says He knows us and that we know Him too. He says this intimate relationship is just like the one He has with the Father.

Jesus is using the deep, intimate relationship the Son has with the Father as a picture of what we can have with Him. This is not a surface-level acknowledgement that we are in the sheepfold or that we're just barely saved. This is the promise that we are one with the Eternal One.

Before we leave John 10, let's look at verse 10:

My sheep **hear** my voice, and **I know** them, and they follow me.

My sheep **listen** to my voice; **I know** them, and they follow me. (NLT)

You can see from this verse that the ones who hear His voice are intimate with Him. 'This also goes both ways: As we hear Him, we get closer to Him. As we become more intimate with Him, we hear Him more. This verse promises that we can hear and recognize the voice of our Beloved.

Be with Him

Being intimate with Jesus is both a status and a process. Look at what Paul says in 1 Corinthians 13:12:

For now we see through a glass, darkly; but then face to face: **now I know in part**; but then shall I know even as also I am known.

Now we see things imperfectly, like puzzling reflections in a mirror, but then we will see everything with perfect clarity. **All that I know now is partial and incomplete**, but then I will know everything completely, just as God now knows me completely. (NLT)

Only the first "know" comes from the Greek word that refers to the intimacy we're talking about. Right now, we "know [or are intimate] in part." But "then"—in the future, when He comes again—we will become fully acquainted and accurately and completely know Him. We are one with Jesus now, but we still see Him and His ways dimly. We are fully intimate with Him but only partially perceive how and what He does.

Be One with Him

We have been looking at the word know in light of having a close relationship with Jesus. But let's look at a different way it is used in the Book of Acts.

Paul had been demonstrating the power of God everywhere he went. Acts 19:11–12 says, "Now God worked unusual miracles by the hands of Paul, so that even handkerchiefs or aprons were brought from his body to the sick, and the diseases left them, and the evil spirits went out of them" (NKJV). But there were some men who tried to copy Paul and cast out demons as he did. On one occasion, seven full-grown men were attacked by one demon-possessed man. Verse 15 says,

> And the evil spirit answered and said, **Jesus I know**, and Paul I know; but who are ye?
>
> But one time when they tried it, the evil spirit replied, "**I know Jesus**, and I know Paul, but who are you?" (NLT)
>
> But one time an evil spirit said to them, "**I know Jesus**, and I know about Paul, but who are you?" (NCV)

When I first read this verse, it caught me off guard a little. And seeing the "know" phrase that I put in bold may catch you off guard as well. First, look at how the New Century Version handles the repeat of the word "know." The spirit said, "I know Jesus." But then it says, "I know about Paul" (italics mine). This shows us that the original Greek word is not the same. Only the first one is the "know" that we're studying in this section.

In light of the word *know*, meaning to experience a close relationship with Jesus, look at how the evil spirit answered: "Jesus I know" or Jesus I have been close to, but Paul I am only acquainted with. What? How can an evil spirit be (or have been) close to Jesus? I believe this level of closeness occurred before Adam fell. There is much teaching about how one-third of the angels followed after Lucifer, were cast out of heaven, and became the evil spirits that Jesus and the rest of the church have had to contend with.

Considering this, we can only be amazed when we think of heaven and the "oneness" that must be there. If spirits—after being cast out of His presence—could still remember being with Him, how much more do the angels now experience it? And how much more can we?

If we backtrack in our list of "know" verses, we can see that the first use of this Greek word *ginōskō* refers to the physical relationship between Joseph and Mary. And the writers of the New Testament used it again and again whenever they talked about having an intimate knowledge of someone.

I have found that when I teach about this level of intimacy, the people who seem the most uncomfortable are the men. I understand, of course. Comparing the oneness with Him with the oneness we achieve when we come together with our spouse—well, I had to seek God about it myself. But as He continued to show me the depth of His feelings for me, my feelings for Him continued to grow, and it reminded me of that newlywed experience I mentioned earlier in this chapter.

You want to be around that person all day, every day. You would do anything to be in their presence. To hold their hand. To be face-to-face. And not just for a few minutes, but for every moment of every day.

> For we are members of his body, of his flesh, and of his bones. For this cause shall a man . . . be joined unto his wife, and they two shall be one flesh. This is a great mystery: but I speak concerning Christ and the church.
>
> Ephesians 5:30–32

This is what God has given us when we say yes to a relationship with Jesus Christ: the opportunity to have an intimate, face-to-face relationship, where there is no holding back from one another. It's all or nothing. I've seen the "nothing" side, and I'll never go back. I choose all!

Have a Personal Relationship with Him

During my first year of Bible college, one of my instructors spoke of having a personal relationship with each Person of the Trinity. At that time, I was only one year out from my back-row experience with the Lord, so I was open to everything, but I also felt free to question things. I thought to myself, "Lord, is this true? Can a person have a relationship with all three Persons of the Godhead?"

I started researching Scripture for myself and found that it was absolutely true! We can have a personal relationship with each Person of the Trinity. And as I have gotten more revelation about this, I have learned that the oneness Their relationship reflects actually mirrors the same type of relationship They want to have with us!' I have applied this truth to my own life, but what does it mean for you? It means Father God wants to have an intimate relationship with you. Jesus wants an intimate relationship with you. And Holy Spirit wants an intimate relationship with you.

Before we go on, I want to address something I have heard a lot when I share this truth. Some people say that they feel "funny" praying to the Father or Holy Spirit. We get so used to saying, "Dear God . . ." or "in Jesus' name, amen," that we forget to recognize the Person—or Persons—we're praying to. Even though prayer simply means having a conversation with someone, I had my own struggles with getting used to talking to the Godhead as individuals.

For days and days, I had to say out loud, to the Father, "I love You, and You love me; I love You, and You love me" over and over, until I felt fully comfortable with having a relationship with Him, my Father. And then I had to do the same with Holy Spirit. Over and over. Now that I'm through that awkwardness, there is no looking back! No turning back. I am fully in love with Them, and They are fully in love with me. I understand that now!

Look at how God, the Creator, reveals Himself in the first chapter of the first letter to the church. Romans 1:20 says,

> For the invisible things of him from the creation of the world are clearly seen, being understood by the things that are made, even **his eternal power and Godhead**; so that they are without excuse.
>
> For ever since the world was created, people have seen the earth and sky. Through everything God made, they can clearly see his invisible qualities—**his eternal power and divine nature**. So they have no excuse for not knowing God. (NLT)
>
> The invisible things about Him—**His eternal power and deity**—have been clearly seen since the creation of the world and are understood by the things that are made, so that they are without excuse. (MEV)

God has made the invisible visible; He has made the invisible clear to His creation so that we can understand Him and see Him and so that we can partake of Him—of Them. God set things up so that we could seek Him and have a relationship with Him—the full Godhead, and then, we in turn can reflect Him without excuse.

Now, let's see what the Bible says about each member of the Godhead so we can get to know them individually and learn more about their unique qualities.

Meet God the Father

> And they heard the sound of the LORD God walking in the garden in the cool of the day, and Adam and his wife hid themselves from the presence of the LORD God among the trees of the garden.
>
> Genesis 3:8 NKJV

Even though this verse is about what happened after the fall, when Adam and Eve tried to hide from God, this verse also gives us a clue to what life was like before. "They heard the sound of . . . God walking." They knew that sound. And He was there "in the cool of the day"; the NASB95 calls it "the time of the evening breeze." It was the time people might think of as being the most comfortable time to sit and hang out with the people you love. God would come down daily—He made it a point to spend intimate time with His creation. And His creation knew Him. They knew the sound of His walk. What a beautiful relationship to have with the Creator.

But to Adam and Eve, God was much more than their Creator. He was their Father! Luke explains this in His genealogy of Jesus. Luke 3:8 starts the list with: "Jesus was known as the son of Joseph," and verse 38 ends it with: "Adam was the son of God" (NLT). Most translations I looked at give this similar phrasing. Jesus was called Joseph's son, and Adam was called the son of God. We're not going to get into the "only begotten" nature of Jesus. I just want you to see that Adam wasn't just God's creation, something like one of earth's animals. God created him and considered him a son.

Adam fell, and now, for centuries, Father has been wanting us back.

> And all things are of God, who hath **reconciled us to himself** by Jesus Christ, and hath given to us the ministry of reconciliation.
>
> 2 Corinthians 5:18

And all of this is a gift from God, who **brought us back to himself** through Christ. And God has given us this task of reconciling people to him.

2 Corinthians 5:18 NLT

The Father gave us Jesus to bring us to Himself. You can see we are talking about having a relationship with the Father, something He has longed for from the time of creation. He so strongly desires this restoration with us that He was willing to send His Son to make all things right and bring us back to that Father-son or Father-daughter relationship.

Ephesians 1:4–5 puts it like this:

According as he hath chosen us in him before the foundation of the world, that we should be holy and without blame before him in love: **having predestinated us unto the adoption of children** by Jesus Christ to himself, according to the good pleasure of his will.

Even before he made the world, God loved us and chose us in Christ to be holy and without fault in his eyes. **God decided in advance to adopt us into his**

own family by bringing us to himself through Jesus Christ. This is what he wanted to do, and it gave him great pleasure. (NLT)

And Romans 8:16 says,

The Spirit itself beareth witness with our spirit, that **we are the children of God.**

For his Spirit joins with our spirit to affirm that **we are God's children**. (NLT)

The Spirit himself testifies together with our spirit that **we are God's children.** (CSB)

You have His Holy Spirit within you continually saying, "You're a child of God. You're a child of God." Holy Spirit talks to your spirit and reminds you that the Father has made you His own. He wants us to know Him as Father so we can experience love and intimacy with Him.

Meet God the Son

Understanding a relationship with Jesus is easy. He became like us, and though He died, rose again, and then went to heaven, we still see Him as a real person, someone who "gets" us.

And the Word was made flesh, and **dwelt among us**, (and we beheld his glory, the glory as of the only begotten of the Father,) full of grace and truth.

John 1:14

So the Word became human and **made his home among us**. He was full of unfailing love and faithfulness. And we have seen his glory, the glory of the Father's one and only Son.

John 1:14 NLT

Now the Word became flesh and **took up residence among us**. We saw his glory—the glory of the one and only, full of grace and truth, who came from the Father.

John 1:14 NET

Jesus became flesh for many reasons, one being so we would have a God (a Member of the Godhead) we could relate to on a human level. God came down and walked and talked with mankind like He did in the garden. But coming down as a Man, as Jesus, to not only walk and talk as a human but to die as one, too, reveals a love that's beyond words.

Jesus came to live with us, to make His home with us, but He also made it so we could be with Him—more specifically, so we could be in Him. We're familiar with Romans 3:23, which says, "For all have sinned, and come short of the glory of God," but let's look at verse 24:

> Being justified freely by his grace through the redemption **that is in Christ Jesus.**
>
> Being justified [declared free of the guilt of sin, made acceptable to God, and granted eternal life] as a gift by His [precious, undeserved] grace, through the redemption [the payment for our sin] **which is [provided] in Christ Jesus**. (AMP)

We hardly need a reminder that we have fallen short of His glory. This world has a way of pointing that out to us every day. What we do need to remember is the justification and redemption that God, through Jesus, provided for us. And where can we find that redemption? *In Him.* In Jesus Christ. The Father freely justified us as His gift to us, and He did that through the redemption that He placed in Jesus.

So, if a right relationship with the Father is held in and through the Son, it would make sense that we should—we must—take the time to get to know Him.

Let's look at a few more passages that have to do with knowing Jesus.

1 Corinthians 1:9 says,

> God is faithful, by whom you were **called into the fellowship of His Son**, Jesus Christ our Lord. (NKJV)
>
> God is faithful, by whom you were **called into fellowship with his son**, Jesus Christ our Lord. (NET)
>
> God will do this, for he is faithful to do what he says, and **he has invited you into partnership with his Son**, Jesus Christ our Lord. (NLT)

"Fellowship" may sound a bit churchy, like a term relegated to a church group or church building. But here, it is related to intimacy with Him. These verses show that we have been called or invited into fellowship or partnership—communion—with Jesus Christ.

Like Paul's longing found in Philippians 3:10, it can become our deepest desire to know Him more:

> **That I may know him**, and the power of his resurrection, and the fellowship of his sufferings, being made conformable unto his death.
>
> **I want to know Christ** and the power that raised him from the dead. I want to share in his sufferings and become like him in his death. (NCV)

Knowing Him and wanting to know Him shows up so many times throughout Scripture; you'll probably start seeing it now every time you read the Bible. Here, Paul desired to know Jesus and build a more intimate relationship with Him so that Paul could—what? So he could "know the power" that's in His resurrection, the power that raised Jesus from the dead and to know how that power works in us and what that power does for and in us.

Let's wrap up this section with 1 John 4:9:

In this the love of God was manifested toward us, that God has sent His only begotten Son into the world, that we might **live through Him**. (NKJV)

God showed how much he loved us by sending his one and only Son into the world so that we might have **eternal life through him**. (NLT)

When talking about the love of God and the intimacy He desires to have with us, it always comes back to John, the beloved disciple or the one "whom Jesus loved." Here John reminds us that God sending Jesus is proof of His love for us, but that isn't the end of the story. He sent Jesus so that we could "live through Him" or "have eternal life through him." Think back to John 17:3, which says, "And this is eternal life, that they may know You, the only true God, and Jesus Christ whom You have sent" (NASB). The very definition of "eternal life" is knowing Him.

What an opportunity and a gift to be able to live in and through the Son. To know Him and the power of His resurrection. To be called into partnership with Him . . .

It's difficult to move on because I want to keep talking about Him. But thank God for Holy Ghost. We'll get to know Him next.

Meet God the Holy Spirit

> If you then, being evil, know how to **give good gifts** to your children, **how much more** will your heavenly Father **give the Holy Spirit** to those who ask Him!
>
> Luke 11:13 NKJV

> So if you sinful people know how to **give good gifts** to your children, **how much more** will your heavenly Father **give the Holy Spirit** to those who ask him.
>
> Luke 11:13 NLT

Our giving Father is pleased to give us His Holy Spirit. In fact, He calls Holy Spirit a "much more" gift! Think about this: Jesus is the one who spoke these words in Luke 11:13. Jesus—the ultimate gift of God! He is proof of the greatness of the Father's gifts. And now, He tells us of another gift, God Himself. Holy Spirit is God. He isn't a thing; He's a Person. Such a magnificent Person. And we can converse with Him.

One day, when I was in prayer, I was telling the Lord how much I loved Him and loved getting to know Him. I was excited to be on this relationship journey and maybe even a little overzealous, but if the Lord has given me something, I want it, and I want it all. So I asked, "How can I get to know You more?"

I will never forget His reply: "Get to know the One with you now. He will speak of me."

I have learned that intimacy with Holy Spirit is vital to my—our—survival in this age that we're living in. We need Him, which is why He promises, "I will never leave you and I will never abandon you" (Heb. 13:5 NET).

Jesus told His disciples that the Father will "give the Holy Spirit to those who ask him," and now John 14:16–17 is where Jesus makes the actual promise of this gift:

> And I will pray the Father, and he shall give you another Comforter, that **he may abide with you for ever**; even the Spirit of truth; whom the world cannot receive, because it seeth him not, neither knoweth him: but **ye know him; for he dwelleth with you, and shall be in you**.

> And I will ask the Father, and he will give you another Advocate, **who will never leave you**. He is the Holy Spirit, who leads into all truth. The world cannot receive him, because it isn't looking for him and doesn't recognize him. But **you know him, because he lives with you now and later will be in you**. (NLT)

Jesus was only hours away from the cross, and He said He would pray for the Father to send us comfort. In anticipation of the worst moment in all of eternity, the Father and the Son still gave. They knew the intimacy that Holy Spirit would bring to our relationship with the whole Godhead. They longed for this intimacy with you and me. So it pleased them to send Him to be with us and in us.

Now, let's look at life after the cross, which is where you and I live.

> Or do you not know that **your body is the temple of the Holy Spirit who is in you**, whom you have from God, and you are not your own?
>
> 1 Corinthians 6:19 NKJV

You should know that **your body is a temple for the Holy Spirit who is in you**. You have received the Holy Spirit from God. So you do not belong to yourselves,

1 Corinthians 6:19 NCV

Haven't you yet learned that **your body is the home of the Holy Spirit God** gave you, and that **he lives within you**? Your own body does not belong to you.

1 Corinthians 6:19 TLB

In John 4:15 (NKJV), Jesus told us, "Abide in Me, and I in you," but then He made sure that would actually happen by sending us His Spirit. Holy Spirit now lives in us and even calls us His temple or His home. He takes such ownership, in fact, that He even tells us that we are not our own anymore. We have given ourselves to Him, and He has been given to us. It sounds a lot like a marriage, the most intimate relationship a person can have, doesn't it.

Some people have had difficulty submitting to Holy Spirit in their lives. Some are a little uneasy with certain aspects of Him. Maybe it's because of things they've heard happening at "that church down the street." Or maybe it's because they just don't see Him as God. They don't understand His presence or His purpose. Second Corinthians 3:17–18 tells us,

Now **the Lord is that Spirit**: and where the Spirit of the Lord is, there is liberty. But we all, with open face beholding as in a glass the glory of the Lord, are changed into the same image from glory to glory, **even as by the Spirit of the Lord**.

For **the Lord is the Spirit**, and wherever the Spirit of the Lord is, there is freedom. So all of us who have had that veil removed can see and reflect the glory of the Lord. And **the Lord—who is the Spirit**—makes us more and more like him as we are changed into his glorious image. (NLT)

We can see right here that the Lord is the Spirit. And in case we didn't understand it in verse 17, He says it again in the next verse. It's obvious that he really wants us to get this. The Lord is Holy Spirit, and Holy Spirit is the Lord.

And look at what He promises us: we are free, and we reflect Him. Where His Spirit lives (which we know is in us!) is a place of freedom. He's continually calling us close and continually setting us free, continually calling us close and continually setting us free. This freedom is non-negotiable. If He is in you, you are free. And He makes you "more and more like him as [you] are changed into his glorious image."

But this freedom and this change come only by the power of Holy Spirit. We need the back-and-forth—He in us and we in Him—to experience His power. We need to see Him as a Person, and we need to get comfortable in His presence.

Right now, God has an opportunity for you—an opportunity to say yes to having a deeper relationship with Jesus. Would you like to get to know him more? You can do that today. Let's move on to our Intimacy Activation Prayer and Practice His Presence.

Intimacy Activation Prayer

Pray your own words or use what I have here. But let's put off the old mindset and put on the new.

God, I want to know you. I want to know every part of You. I want to know You as my Father, I want to know Your Son, and I want to know Your precious Spirit. Help me know more of You, more of Your Presence, more of Your fullness and more of Your glory in my life.

I encourage you to pray this prayer or a version of it several times a day for the next week. Pray it when you wake up, before a prayer session, before Bible study or devotional time, or on your way to work—pray it anytime! Watch your awareness of His desire for intimacy with you grow.

Practice His Presence

In the next chapter, we will get into the fundamentals of your regular practice of His presence. But to close out this chapter, I wanted to present some of my own personal prayers to the Lord. Feel free to use them or pray your own. Notice, though, that these prayers are based on Scripture. Jesus is the Word made flesh, so I know that when I pray His word, I am always praying in line with His will. Keep that in mind if you ever struggle with finding words to say to Him.

The following is an example of how I might pray distinctly with the Father; it is based on Ephesians 1:4–5: "According as he hath chosen us in him before the foundation of the world, that we should be holy and without blame before him in love: having predestinated us unto the adoption of children by Jesus Christ to himself, according to the good pleasure of his will."

Father, I thank You that You chose me. You knew that humanity would deny You, yet You still chose to proceed with us. You so wanted me in Your life that You said yes to Jesus going to the cross before the foundation of the earth was laid. Your most beautiful, prized possession was given for me. I thank You that Jesus made me right with You. He switched places with me so I could be adopted into Your family. Forever adopted, to never be separated. Jesus so desired that You and I have relationship, conversation, and restoration. You, the Creator and Sustainer of all things, want to have a one-on-one relationship with me. What a beautiful picture You paint for me, Lord, as I close my eyes and think on these truths. Like the father of the prodigal son,

You were the Father anticipating my return. Constantly watching in expectation for me to make my way to You. Waiting for the hug, the kiss, the party! Thank You, Father, for the elaborate rescue mission and for Your unfailing and unending love. Holy Father, Wonderful Maker, I thank and love You.

This next example is how I might commune distinctly with Jesus, the Son. This prayer is based on John 1:14: "And the Word was made flesh, and dwelt among us, (and we beheld his glory, the glory as of the only begotten of the Father,) full of grace and truth."

Jesus, I love You so much. It's an amazing thought that You would come down from the heavens and take up residence with Your creation. That alone is astounding! Yet You knew beforehand that You would go to the cross for us. Incredible! It's hard to wrap my mind around someone so bursting with love. Not only did You leave the wonderful place You call home, but You accepted coming into this world as a baby. The Maker of the heavens and earth sat patiently in a woman's womb for nine months! The Lifeforce of the universe in a human's belly. The Designer of the process came through the process just so You could be one of us.

Jesus, I am awestruck by Your humility. Your life speaks so loudly of humility and meekness. I praise Your name, Messiah. I praise Your name, my King. Thank You for giving everything up for me, for walking among us and showing us Your glory. The Son who is truly unique, who is one of a kind, I praise Your name and worship You.

Now, this next example is how I might pray to Holy Spirit, based on John 16:13: "Howbeit when he, the Spirit of truth, is come, he will guide you into all truth: for he shall not speak of himself; but whatsoever he shall hear, that shall he speak: and he will shew you things to come."

Holy Spirit, I see these words written in red in my Bible, so this is my Lord and Master, Jesus, speaking to me. Jesus was so excited for You to come! He knew how important Your role as the Spirit of Truth was going to be to me. Jesus says that when You come, You will lead me into all truth. So Your job isn't selfish or self-centered, You're not making it all about You. You get to come and lead me into all truth. Hallelujah! You are someone who doesn't speak of Himself, and You are constantly revealing truth to me. You are for me. I praise Your name, Holy Spirit, and thank You for the heart You have for Jesus. John 16:13 says that You won't speak of Yourself, but You only speak what You hear—that's what You will speak. You remind me of Jesus and the amount of humility He walked in. Jesus was constantly speaking of the Father, and You are constantly speaking of the Son. You're all three so wonderful! One is always speaking and pointing to the other, always magnifying each other. I thank You, Holy Spirit. You are so good. Keep speaking, and I will keep listening. Have patience with me as I grow. I know You will never give up on me. You'll always be with me and always be for me. Thank You, Holy Ghost.

Chapter 2
Spending Time Alone with Him
Practicing His Presence

*The one thing I ask of the Lord—**the thing I seek most**—is to live in the house of the Lord all the days of my life, delighting in the Lord's perfections and meditating in his Temple. For **he will conceal me there when troubles come**; he will hide me in his sanctuary. He will place me out of reach on a high rock.*

Psalm 27:4–5 NLT

Even though I grew up in church, I hadn't given my heart fully to the Lord until I was an adult. During that back-row experience, I had come to the end of myself, my past was my past, and God forever changed my present and my future. When God showed up so spectacularly, I "saw" Him. I "heard" Him. I can't say that I saw His face, and I didn't hear an audible voice, but I perceived His heart. He showed me things about my past, present, and future. And He showed me the love He has for me, for my family, and for His children—the believers I was surrounded by at that very moment and those whom I will meet in the future. The only way I can describe this perception of His heart is that it was burned into everything that I am or will be.

Even after He had shared so much with me, I still couldn't get enough. I wanted more. I told the Lord that I would not be mediocre. And I would do whatever it took to never live in mediocrity. I didn't know what that kind of commitment looked like, but I didn't care. I wanted to be everything He desired me to be. So, when He said, "Just sit with Me," I thought it seemed too simple.

But I learned quickly how powerful His instructions could be.

See Him and Be Changed

Exodus 33:20 records the words that God said to Moses when Moses asked to see His glory: "You cannot see My face, for no man can see Me and live!" (NASB95).

From the previous chapter, we saw how Adam and Even had an intimate relationship with God. We don't know how long they were in the garden before they sinned and were cast out, but they had obviously spent enough time with Him to recognize the sound of His walking. They saw Him daily, yet they did not die from seeing Him.

So maybe when sin entered their lives, they could no longer see Him. That's what we have been taught. But think about it, after they ate the fruit, they hid from God, but did God hide from them? There was conversation and several events after the fall. God called to Adam; Adam answered. God talked to Eve; she spoke back. The man blamed the woman; the woman blamed the snake. God issued a series of curses: the serpent, the woman's childbearing, the ground. God made clothes for Adam and Eve out of the skins of animals. After making the clothes, the Bible says that "the LORD God . . . *clothed* them . . . *sent* him out of the garden . . . He *drove* out the man" (Gen. 3:21, 23–24 NKJV, italics added).

Look at all that happened after the fall—after sin entered into man's life. There was still some back and forth between God and humans. Maybe, because of shame, they didn't look God in the face, but you have to imagine that they saw Him somehow. Genesis 5:5 tells us that Adam lived to be 930 years old. In the garden, it was *sin* that caused man's life clock to start ticking down; it wasn't looking at God.

So back to Moses's question about wanting to see God's glory. God said that His face could not be seen, but He did not deny Moses's request, which was to see God's "glorious presence" (Ex. 33:18 NLT). God set Moses in an opening in the side of the mountain, gently placed His hand over him, and then passed by him.

Moses experienced God's glorious presence, and lived to tell about it.

What I want you to see is that even in man's sinful state, God *wanted* to be seen and known. And He always found a way to make that happen. In fact, a few verses before the Moses-God interaction, the Bible says, "The LORD would speak to Moses face to face, as one speaks to a friend" (Ex. 33:11 NLT). This was an ongoing event, something that Moses had lived to talk about.

If Adam and Moses didn't die physically when they spent time with the Lord, why do so many believers today think that God keeps His distance from us now? Sometimes people think that a sin or multiple sins they've committed means they can't enter His presence. But that's just not the case. (We'll talk more about His presence and why we might feel a withdrawing of sorts in chapters 3 and 4.)

Other Old Testament people (before Jesus and the cross!) saw God in one form or another and lived: Abraham saw and talked with God too many times to count (example, Gen. 18). Jacob wrestled with God and limped away (Gen. 32:22–30). Gideon met Him while secretly processing wheat in a winepress (Judg. 6:11–12). Isaiah saw Him sitting on a throne when he was called to be a prophet (Isa. 6:1). And Shadrach, Meshach, and Abednego were joined by a fourth firewalker in the furnace, and King Nebuchadnezzar saw Him (Dan. 3:8–29).

There are so many more examples of Old Testament people who saw God and lived. But these people didn't just see Him and live. They saw Him and were changed! So when the Old Testament verse says, "No man can see Me and live" (Ex. 33:20 NASB95), maybe we New Testament folks can read it differently. What if that verse could be understood as "no one can see Him and walk away *unchanged*"?

Think about how after the fall, mankind was destined to die. But after Jesus's death and resurrection, mankind—all who believe on Him—are brought to new life. If Old Testament people who saw Him were changed, how much more can *we* expect to be changed when we see Him—when we enter His presence?

This is an invitation to come away with Him and be forever marked by Him.

Hear Him and Live

I mentioned earlier in this chapter that when I experienced the presence of God while in the back row of that church, I heard Him speak to me. I said it wasn't an audible voice, but it was such a strong perception in my heart that it might as well have been audible. Sometimes people can't get past the strangeness of thinking that

God still speaks today. I think that is because they can only think of a voice they can hear with their ears.

Just like God appeared in different forms to the Old Testament people we talked about in the last section, God also speaks differently to different people. He will talk to you in the way that *you* can understand. Be open and expectant. And hear Him.

His voice is so precious. His voice is enough. When He speaks, all stand still. We in the church have put such an emphasis on that "still small voice" or a whisper (1 Kin. 19:12) that I fear we have minimized the mighty power and ability our God has to speak.

Psalm 68:33 declares that God has a "thundering" and "mighty voice"!

> To him that rideth upon the heavens of heavens, which were of old; lo, he doth send out his voice, and that a **mighty voice**.
>
> To him who rides upon the ancient heavens, whose **mighty voice thunders** from the sky. (TLB)
>
> Sing to the one who rides through the skies, which are from long ago. He speaks with a **thundering voice**. (NCV)

This verse is interesting to study in various translations because of the combining or interchanging of the words *mighty* and *thunder*. It is a similar description to what happened after Jesus was baptized. Scripture says that when He was brought up out of the water, God spoke. And what did the people hear?

> The crowd that stood there and **heard the voice said that it had thundered**. Others said that an angel had spoken to him.
>
> John 12:29 NET
>
> When the crowd **heard the voice**, some of them **thought it was thunder**, while others declared an angel had spoken to him.
>
> John 12:29 TLB

God has been speaking for centuries. We see in the first chapter of Genesis that God spoke during creation. He spoke beautiful, full sentences that contained purpose and direction. Later in the same book, God gave Noah very specific, detailed instructions on how to build the ark and who and what to bring. In Exodus, God gave Moses instructions on building His tabernacle and conducting worship in it, down to the finest, most exact detail. From the type and color of fabric for the curtains and the priestly clothing to the spices and oil to use for the anointing oil to the kind of wood, precious metals, and gems to use for the furniture and accessories—God spoke in detail and with precision.

He has never stopped speaking to His creation, and He speaks with the same precision, purpose, and care today as He has throughout history.

The tabernacle of the old covenant was eventually put aside for the temple that Solomon built, which later was also put aside when it was destroyed. The tabernacle and the temple were always intended to be temporary. But how great and better is our new covenant? God has created a new home—new homes!—and He moved inside them. When we accepted Him, He recreated us and turned each of us into a spotless home for Holy Spirit. First Corinthians 3:16 asks, "Do you not know that you are God's temple and that God's Spirit lives in you?" (NET).

What holy communion. What a perfect union. *That's* intimacy.

Intimacy Activation Prayer

Pray your own words or use what I have here. Read over it once to get familiar with it, then pray it over yourself. Speak it over your life. Now, let's pray and put off the old mindset and put on the new.

Lord, help me. You've been speaking for centuries. Help me hear You now. Help me take You out of the box that man has put You in. I will say what Your word says. I will speak over my life what the Bible says. I choose this truth: the God who speaks with a mighty thundering voice is with me now. You live in me. And You are never against me, but You are forever for me.

Find Your Quiet Place

"Sometimes when I'm going somewhere and I wait, a somewhere comes to me."

—Winnie the Pooh

You may have been expecting Scripture right there and not a quote by a child's storybook character. But Jesus did say to come to Him as little children (see Matt. 18:3). Sometimes the simplest statement can have a big impact. This one describes my early experiences of sitting with Jesus, and maybe it will describe yours too.

For the rest of this chapter, I will be preparing you for your first "official" prayer closet time or sit-with-Him time or whatever you want to call it.

As soon as I got saved, I got hungry for God. And I don't mean a light stomach growl, I-want-a-sandwich kind of hungry. I mean, I was famished! As soon as I began to partake of Him, I never stopped. I couldn't get enough, and I still can't. I read the Bible, listened to it on audio, heard sermons both at church and away, and I read books by great teachers of the word, some of them still alive, some gone. When I read from these teachers, something I kept seeing was how they talked about their time in their prayer closet or simply their alone time with God.

These teachers were also powerful. They got revelations from the word of God, they preached life-changing sermons, and they were used to perform healings and miracles. I couldn't help seeing a modern parallel to how Jesus would go away by Himself to pray and come back ready to teach and to heal.

I knew there was something to this "closet," or inward, prayer life. I was hungry for God, but I was also busy. I knew those powerful teachers had also been busy, yet they spent hours in prayer—daily. I wondered how a person could pray for hours like that. Do they fall asleep? Do they run out of things to say? Would I?

I am happy to tell you that God understands our concerns. He understood mine, and He didn't leave me alone to figure things out. He helped me. And He will help you too. The key is just to do it. I didn't start out able to pray for hours—even with God helping me. And I'm pretty sure those powerful teachers of God didn't start out with hours either. We all have to grow into it.

Maybe even Jesus started out small. The first time in the Bible that we see Jesus speak is when He was twelve years old and had spent hours in the Father's house. And then we don't see Him again for another eighteen years. During this time, He grew in His relationship with the Father. I'm convinced that He knows and understands the time and growth that needs to take place for each of us.

But is your desire to know Him there? Are you ready to step into more intimacy with Him? I'm going to share some practical steps you can take and tips to get you started. These are what worked for me, and they might work for you. But you need to remember two things. First, you have to actually go do it—go pray. And second, remember that He wants to be with you so much that He will lead you to the steps that will work best for you. Those steps might include what I'm about to share, or they might be completely, personally your own.

Here's a brief list of items you might want to start with as you begin your practice:

1. A room or closet where you can experience quiet and be alone
2. A towel, floor pillow, foam mat, etc.
3. A timer of some sort that's not your phone
4. A journal, notebook, or blank paper and pen or pencil
5. One or two Scriptures written out on paper, in your journal, or on an index card

Notice what's missing from this list: technology (like your phone) and a Bible. Don't worry; I'll explain.

When I first started locking myself away with the Lord, I did a few things to help myself be successful. I decided I would pray on my knees as a way to train my mind and my body to recognize this as prayer time. I found that a folded-up towel really helps on both carpeted and hard floors. I had a timer that I set for five minutes. (Although I'm starting you with two minutes, you can do more if you want to.) My goal was to see how long I could last in a room alone with the Lord and how long I could be on my knees before Him.

During those times, I would close my eyes and just talk with Him, adore Him, say what the Bible says about Him, and so on. As I built up stamina on my knees in my prayer closet, I noticed my vocabulary, my ability to say different things to Him, grew as well. At that point, I would move the timer to ten minutes and practice that for a few days. As I felt led to, I would then move the timer up even more.

Practicing this way was important to me. Mainly because I like to see tangible results sometimes, so tracking my time was helpful. This method showed me day-by-day how I was improving. And it wasn't just helping me see the physical side of improvement but also the spiritual side, which was what I was most after.

In your own practice, make sure you can find a place where you can be alone and away from distractions. Even though that is easier said than done, if you truly want to grow in intimacy with the Lord, you will have to make this happen somehow.

If you choose to kneel, be sure to have something comfortable to kneel on. I would discourage sitting back in a chair or on a couch or lying down, especially early on. It's too easy to fall asleep or let your mind wander. Being on our knees is a foreign position and even a little uncomfortable, so it helps keep us engaged.

However, we're not going for pain, which is why I recommend a towel or floor pillow or a mat.

As for the timer—I said no technology, yet many of us use our phones for our clocks, alarms, and timers. If there is any way you can avoid bringing a phone into your closet with you, I would urge you to do so. Some ideas of what you can use instead might be a digital timer, an actual clock, or even an hourglass. Another idea is to set the alarm on a bedroom clock, a computer, or your phone in the room outside your prayer closet. The only problem with this, though, is if your alarm needs to be turned off manually, it might interrupt times when you want to pray past the designated timeframe. If you must use your phone, placing it in airplane mode could be an option. Use your imagination and be creative. But make it your goal to avoid outside distractions at all costs.

Get Your Prayer Journal

Next, I want to focus on one of the most important tools you can bring with you into your prayer closet: a notebook or journal (and, of course, something to write with). I didn't start off my alone time practice with jotting things down in a prayer journal. Using a journal is something I picked up over time, but I wish I had started it from the beginning. I would urge you not to skip this valuable tool.

If you are in the practice of keeping a daily journal or diary, then I would suggest you use a different book for your prayer time. Your prayer journal shouldn't function as a daily log of your activities or appointments. For that reason, a hardcopy book versus a digital document is what I recommend. Your journal is intended to be used for two specific purposes.

The first way you may use your journal, especially early on, is to jot things down that are on your mind and keeping you from focusing on God. This should help you, especially if you're a task-oriented person. When you go into your prayer room, we may have a lot on our minds. Sometimes our minds are racing with to-do lists, job tasks, household chores, grocery lists, etc. You may start your prayer time strong—you're worshiping, praying in the Spirit, reading your favorite Bible verse, singing a praise song—when you suddenly remember an email you forgot to send, or you start planning your dinner. This is the time to use your journal. Jot down that random thought if it's something you need to remember for later. Then get back to praying.

Of course, you probably already know that won't be the end of those random thoughts. When another task comes to mind, write it down, and then go back to praying. It's only natural that our minds wander—for now—but since we're looking to move into the spiritual and out of the natural, we need to do what it takes to get to that point. Writing down those "urgent" thoughts actually gets them out of your mind for the time being. Writing a thought down means you can forget about it for now, but you have record of it for when you are out of your prayer room and in a position to actually take care of it.

On a side note, although it is "natural" that our minds wander in these early stages, I believe we were made for Him. Our original design included the ability to focus on Him. We were made to look at Him and not be distracted and not look away. Practicing redirection in prayer time helps realign your soul back to its original state, which is a state of constant communion with the One who lovingly created you.

Over time you will see that you are training your mind to hush up while you wait in the beautiful presence of the Lord. Early on, I literally told my mind, "Okay, you only get a couple of times to distract me with these thoughts, and then you're done, and I'm all His." Saying this and things like it was a way to coach myself and redirect my thoughts back to the reason I was in there in the first place. But to tell you the truth, I only had to do this for a few months. Through this practice, I was able to train my mind and flesh to quiet down during my alone times with the Lord.

The second and more important reason to bring paper and pen with you is that it becomes part of your back-and-forth conversation with Him. Our prayer time should not be seen as us just talking at Him and pouring our hearts out to Him and then we're done. Conversation goes two ways. And so does your journal—you can write your prayers to Him, and you can record what He says to you.

What this does for your prayer time is it creates an atmosphere of faith and expectancy. When you bring paper and pen into the equation, you are declaring that He *is* going to speak to you, and you *will* hear Him.

Think about the following verses:

But without faith it is impossible to please Him, for he who comes to God must believe that He is, and that He is a rewarder of those who diligently seek Him.

Hebrews 11:6 NKJV

My sheep hear My voice, and I know them, and they follow Me.

John 10:27 NKJV

Bringing a journal or notebook into your prayer closet with you seems like such a simple step, and it is. But it's a step of faith. So try not to skip this step.

Writing down what you hear during your prayer time will give you something that you can track over time. This has been an amazing practice for me, because even though things started out slowly, God started speaking to me so frequently and to such lengths that I couldn't keep up at times. (Something that you can look forward to for yourself!)

Now I can look back in my prayer journal and see what He was speaking to me six months ago, a year ago, and more. I can see promises that have come to pass in my life and the things I'm still waiting to see manifest. It also gives me a way to focus or redirect my thoughts toward something I may have missed or maybe something I didn't quite complete with Him. I can look back and see the thoughts He has for me and how He worded those thoughts, such as how He wove Scripture through those encouraging words.

Practice His Presence

Everything we do in terms of communing with the Father, Son, and Holy Ghost should be considered a practice. In practice, there is no failure but only a desire to grow. To grow closer, grow stronger.

When you step into your quiet place, and you're ready to pray, throw off memories or ideas of what prayer time should look like. The prayer time I'm sharing with you is all about intimacy;

you're not praying "typical" prayers. This time is all about speaking sweet nothings to Jesus like you might to a lover. Don't ask Him for anything, and don't pray for anyone. Speak straight to Jesus Himself. Tell Him how much you love Him and what He means to you. Say it out loud. I promise you, Jesus wants to hear you!

So you can see that there is no need for eloquence, no need to plan your words or try to be poetic, here's an example of what I may say:

Jesus, I love You.

I thank You.

There's no one like You.

Thank You, Jesus.

You make all things right.

I praise your name, Jesus.

You calm me down when I'm feeling crazy.

You love everyone, Beautiful Savior.

You're after everyone, Jesus.

The Father was pleased to put everything in You, so people could come to You.

Holy Spirit, I thank You for being here.

Thank You, Holy Spirit.

Thank You for Your love and affection.

Thank You for constantly transforming me into the image of the Son.

Thank you, Jesus.

I thank You that there's no fear in You.

Everything about You is love.

You defeated fear, and it's a complete defeat, a total victory.

You are victorious.

Your name is Victorious.

You are the King.

You wear the crown.

You hold the glory.

I praise your name, Jesus.

I thank You for Your love.

I thank You for your Son, Father.

I thank You for Your willingness and obedience.

I thank You, Jesus, for everything You do for me on a daily basis.

I thank You, for what you've done in my past.

I thank You, for what you're doing in my future.

Yours is the Kingdom.

Yours is the glory.

Yours is the honor.

Yours is the majesty.

Thank you, Jesus.

Even though we're talking about your planned prayer time, this type of "sweet nothings" prayer is something you can speak at any point in the day, every day. In fact, I encourage you to do it. You can whisper sweet nothings to Him while you're in a store; you can do this at home or in school. Talk to Him while doing those annoying chores like fixing a flat tire, doing the dishes, or changing a diaper. This type of praying won't necessarily change your *physical* environment, but there is a shift in the atmosphere. A knowing will arise within you that Holy Ghost is alive in you and working on you from the inside out.

Now, it's your turn. Get your notebook or journal and a pen or pencil. Go into your quiet place. Set a timer for two minutes (five max; be willing to start small). Now just whisper little things to Him.

Tell Him what He means to you, what He *is* to you. Adore Him. Don't use this time to ask for anything. Don't pray for others, including yourself, yet. Just love Him. Love *on* Him.

Remember to use your notebook to (1) jot down distracting thoughts to get them out of your mind, and (2) write what you feel God is speaking back to you. When your time ends, take another minute or two to reflect on the experience. What happened? Did you feel a change? Write your thoughts in your notebook. Don't skip this step. It's a great way to track your experiences throughout your prayer practices. Over time, you will have a tangible, written record of your increased connection with Holy Spirit!

Chapter 3

Experiencing His Presence

Understanding Who and Where He Is

One thing have I desired of the Lord, that will I seek after; ***that I may dwell in the house of the Lord*** *all the days of my life,* ***to behold the beauty of the Lord****, and to enquire in his temple. For in the time of trouble he shall hide me in his pavilion: in the secret of his tabernacle shall he hide me; he shall set me up upon a rock.*

Psalm 27:4–5 KJV

Before you start reading this chapter, I hope you have taken the time to work through chapter 2, that you found your quiet place, and that you have experienced some intimate time away with the Lord.

Your Spirit's Power over the Mind and Flesh

You may have confronted distractions of both the mind and the flesh in your prayer times—recently or in the past. And if you can recall, two of the things I suggested you bring into your prayer closet with you were a journal (for the wandering thoughts) and a cushion (for physical comfort). Though these things can help you focus, they are external tools and can only help so much. What you truly need to know is that you have power within yourself to take control in these areas. The power is within you because *He* is in you—"Greater is he that is in you, than he that is in the world" (1 John 4:4).

You may already understand that you are a three-part being. But in case this concept is new to you, let me show you what I mean.

We have talked about the Trinity, about the fact that God is a three-part Being. Since we are made in His image (see Gen. 1:27), it would make sense that we, too, are made up of three parts. First Thessalonians 5:23 leaves no question about this:

> Now may the God of peace Himself sanctify you entirely; and may your **spirit and soul and body be kept complete**, without blame at the coming of our Lord Jesus Christ. (NASB)
>
> Now, may the God of peace and harmony set you apart, making you completely holy. And may **your entire being—spirit, soul, and body**—be kept completely flawless in the appearing of our Lord Jesus, the Anointed One. (TPT)

I studied several translations of this verse, and every one that I looked at made a clear distinction between these three parts: spirit, soul (part of your soul is your mind), and body. But let's look at another verse that isn't as clear-cut as the one in 1 Thessalonians but still reveals all three parts—3 John verse 2:

> Beloved, I pray that in all respects **you** may prosper and be in good **health**, just as your **soul** prospers. (NASB)
>
> Dear friend, I pray that all may go well with **you** and that you may be in good **health**, just as it is well with your **soul**. (NET)
>
> Dear friend, I pray that **you** may enjoy good **health** and that all may go well with you, even as your **soul** is getting along well. (NIV)

Notice the bold words in these verses. I believe the word "you" refers to your *spirit*. If you're born again, your spirit is alive unto God and is the main part of you. Then the word "health" refers to your body. The third word, "soul," wraps this verse up and shows the three distinct parts of a human being.

So, when I say you have power over the mind (soul) and the flesh, I am talking about the power God has put in you to force these parts of you to submit to who is truly in charge, your spirit. This is who you really are. And your spirit man is chomping at the bit to get alone with the One who created you. That part of you is the part who is in perfect union with El Shaddai Himself.

From what we learned in chapter 1, we understand that our *spirit*'s desire is to know Him, so in this section, we're going to talk about the other two parts of us—the mind and flesh—and what we can do to get them to shut up so our spirits can lead our intimate times with Jesus.

There is a lot of teaching that describes the soul as containing our mind, will, and emotions. For the sake of our discussion, I'm just going to refer to this part of us as the mind. And when I talk about taking control of the mind, I'm talking about those thoughts and mental distractions that try to pull our focus off God. When you first start a regular prayer closet practice, these distracting thoughts will probably come on strong, but with regular practice and exercise of your authority over them, over time, they will fade. You can train your mind to be quiet before the Lord. In fact, I believe that with training, this desire to stay in the secret place will become so strong that you just don't want to leave it. And when you do leave, you'll feel a continual pull to go right back.

With training, this desire to stay in the secret place will become so strong that you just don't want to leave it.

Now when I talk about the flesh, I'm talking about the body, and it can refer to a few things. It could be external discomforts like your knees hurting from kneeling or leg cramps or limbs falling asleep or even *all of you* falling asleep. It could be a sickness that you're fighting, so a cough or a headache could keep you from enjoying your prayer time. Flesh distractions could also be internal things like hunger or thirst or even a full bladder! I've experienced a number of these issues, but I have experimented with different ways to address them, and I've learned that there aren't any that can't be overcome. You, too, can overcome them through the power Holy Spirit has given you. Praise God!

I have found five different ways that can help overcome the distractions that can take our attention off Him. They are things you can *do* to train your mind and flesh, but it's important to understand that the power to overcome is given to you by God.

> I say, then, **walk by the Spirit** and **you will certainly not carry out the desire of the flesh**. For the flesh desires what is against the Spirit, and the Spirit desires what is against the flesh; these are opposed to each

other, so that you don't do what you want. But if **you are led by the Spirit**, you are not under the law.

Galatians 5:16–18 CSB

One: Practice. This is the first and possibly the most important thing you can do to train your mind and flesh to be quiet before the Lord. In practice there is no failure, only something learned. If you enter into this process expecting perfection, you will be disappointed. Every wandering thought and every growl of the stomach can make you feel like you're not reaching that preconceived bar. The only things you should expect when you enter your prayer closet are that He *will* show up and that you *will* grow. That's it. As a discipline shifts from duty to delight, you will have peace. But for that to happen, the discipline must be practiced.

See it as a journey, a road you're traveling with the destination being to know Him. Ephesians 3:18 is Paul's prayer that you "will have the power to understand the greatness of Christ's love—**how wide** and **how long** and **how high** and **how deep** that love is" (NCV). Considering those bold phrases, can you see how this isn't a destination at all but a journey that never really ends? Can you also see the ineffectiveness of expecting a specific outcome?

Just practice. Make time with Him a habit. Schedule the time; plan for it; put it on your calendar. Do it on purpose. As you put Him first, you will see how He has already put you first.

Two: Pen and paper. I have already mentioned this one in the last chapter. In the list of tools, it's probably the most practical, but it's not any less important or less spiritual. Second Corinthians 10:5 says that we can "capture every thought and make it give up and obey Christ" (NCV). One way to do that is to write down those stray thoughts. This doesn't have to be full sentences or even legible. Just jot down the random thought to get it out of your brain, and then go right back to what you were doing.

For me, the process of retraining my mind using this method was progressive. When a thought that I didn't want to forget would come, I would jot it down and then go back to meditating or praying or just staying quiet before Him. Sometimes only a few seconds would pass before another thought would come. I jotted that down, too, and then went back to praying. Over the next few weeks, I noticed that the thoughts came less and less. Eventually, I trained my mind to refuse access to distracting thoughts. In fact, I even stopped bringing the extra paper in with me because I just didn't need it anymore. I still bring a journal with me, but that's different from the pen and paper I'm talking about here.

The time this retraining happens for you will vary. We're all at different stages of life, and we all have different concerns. If you find that you never lose the need for this paper tool, that's okay. Remember, it's a journey. But I pray that you experience peace and bliss immediately. And I encourage you to believe for the same!

Three: Redirection. This can be used for both your mind and your flesh, and it is simply directing your thoughts toward His "voice" and away from what is trying to capture your attention. Let me explain. The first thing I mean when I say "voice" involves your expectation of hearing from God during your prayer time. You can prep by bringing in a phrase or a verse of Scripture, written or memorized. When your mind tries to wander, simply say the verse; say it slowly and savor each word. Set your mind and heart up to be expectant. Anticipate hearing from Him. Don't be afraid to expect a vision from Him. Be open to whatever He wants to do. Don't make visions and voices the priority; make *Him* the priority. Just be open to however He chooses to manifest Himself in those moments.

The other way to redirect your mind (and flesh) back to Jesus is by Scripture itself. I'm not talking about using the whole Bible during these times. Bible reading and Bible study are disciplines all their own. Just one scripture will do; He is there in all of them. On an index card or in your journal, write down one or two verses, and bring them into your secret place with you. This will give you a point of focus when your mind starts to wander off. You can change the verse from time to time or use your favorite one as your go-to redirection technique. But like the example in the previous paragraph, speak this verse slowly and savor it. Think on each word. Allow it to captivate your mind until there is no more room for distracting thoughts.

This redirection practice was difficult for me at first because of my love for Scripture. Sometimes when I get into the word, I feel like I just can't get enough of it. But I realized that my quiet time with Him is neither the time nor the place for Bible reading. It's the time and place for seeking and finding Him. It's the place for Him to be the ruler of your time—and your life. This is why I recommend only bringing in one or two verses and not the whole Bible. That amount of Scripture can be a distraction in itself. I'm not saying anything negative about the Bible. Bible reading has its own time and place. But the written word should always lead us to the Living Word, and your secret place is all about being quiet before Him and experiencing His presence. As I have grown in this area, I've been able to bring my Bible into my prayer room and still stick to just one scripture. You may be able to do the same, but to start out with, I suggest writing your verse down and leaving the Bible in the other room.

How I use Scripture to redirect my thoughts is that I say the verse out loud. And I say it in my head. I repeat it in phrases and then as a whole. After I have said it several times, I ask the Lord to reveal things about the verse to me because He is the great Revelator. Through this process of back and forth, we have developed a relationship that we both enjoy. (We will cover this in-depth in chapter 5.)

Four: Close your eyes. This is the simplest one of the four, but it can have a massive impact on helping you control your mind and flesh. We are visual creatures. Closing our eyes shuts off one of our keenest senses, eliminating one entire route of distractions. This can be a fine line between closing your eyes to pray and it causing you to fall asleep, but if practiced enough, it will help you grow the ability to "see" the things of God.

Five: Use your authority. Proverbs 18:21 says, "Death and life are in the power of the tongue." This says that what we say has power over the farthest extremes: life and death. It stands to reason that everything in between would also fall under this power. What you speak in your prayer closet can cause things to happen. So be bold and speak big!

The best way I can illustrate this point is to share something from my personal experience. During one of my times with the Lord, I was practicing silence before Him. I don't know how much time I had been sitting with Him, but I could really feel the presence of Holy Ghost; He was in the room with me. I did not want to leave that special moment. Unfortunately, my bladder had a different idea. I *really* needed to use the restroom. But I was not going to let my flesh interrupt such a special moment with God. I put my finger on my lower abdomen, where I assumed my bladder is located, and I said, "Stop bothering me. You will wait until I'm done. You don't have a choice!" Immediately the pressure and desire to "go" went away! I had used my authority on my flesh, and my flesh obeyed. It was amazing!

This might seem like an awkward example, but it's a very real situation that any of us could experience. And it's important to know that you do not have to bow to the flesh. You have a choice.

Facets of His Presence

So far, we have talked about what intimacy is and what it means to know God as Father, Son, and Holy Spirit. Then you had our first practice or two of sitting with Him and beginning that relationship of intimacy. Next, we discussed how to take charge of your time with Him and not allow your mind and flesh to interrupt your times with Him. Now, I want to talk about God's presence and show you that to focus on Jesus, you need to look no further than within.

If you've been around the things of God for any length of time, you have probably heard that God is omnipresent—He is everywhere all the time. But do we really know what that means? And do we really understand His presence? I thought I did, but as I grew in my practice of sitting quietly with Him, I would clearly sense when He came into the room. Of course, He is always present, but there was a difference in those moments when I felt Him "show up."

I have gotten to know Him well, and I know that He doesn't mind when I question things. In fact, I ask *a lot* of questions. As I grew in this, I questioned everything about His Presence, the who, what, when, where, why, and how. I wondered, Who is the One actually coming into the room at those times when the atmosphere changed? What is it about what I'm doing that brings Him in such a way? What time of day, where am I, and what is the environment at those moments? And can I replicate the details? Does He show up the same way for other people, or is this experience just mine alone?

I want to focus on three different facets of God's presence: the indwelling presence, His omnipresence, and the manifest presence of God.

Who is the One actually coming into the room at those times when the atmosphere changed? What is it about what I'm doing that brings Him in such a way?

The Indwelling Presence of God

The indwelling presence of God is His Holy Spirit dwelling or living in you. This indwelling takes place the very moment you give your life to Jesus.

> Even the Spirit of truth; whom the world cannot receive, because it seeth him not, neither knoweth him: but ye know him; for **he dwelleth with you, and shall be in you**.
>
> John 14:17

1 Corinthians 6:19–20 restates this indwelling by calling our bodies a temple, a dwelling place, of Holy Spirit.

> What? Know ye not that your body is the temple of the **Holy Ghost which is in you**, which ye have of God, and ye are not your own? For ye are bought with a

price: therefore glorify God in your body, and in your spirit, which are God's.

Don't you realize that your body is the temple of the **Holy Spirit, who lives in you** and was given to you by God? You do not belong to yourself for God bought you with a high price. So you must honor God with your body. (NLT)

The indwelling—the permanent living inside you—of God Himself is a gift (not earned by our works) that God has given to His children. Unbelievers don't have this indwelling.

Not by works of righteousness which we have done, but according to his mercy **he saved us**, by the washing of **regeneration**, and **renewing** of the Holy Ghost.

Titus 3:5

But ye are not in the flesh, but in the Spirit, if so be that the Spirit of God dwell in you. Now **if any man have not the Spirit of Christ, he is none of his**. . . . But if the Spirit of him that raised up Jesus from the dead dwells in you, he that raised up Christ from the dead shall also quicken your mortal bodies by his Spirit that dwelleth in you.

Romans 8:9, 11

Again, this indwelling of God means that He lives in you through the person of the Holy Ghost. He has freely given His Spirit to us as a gift. It is His choice to make His home in you!

He has freely given His Spirit to us as a gift. It is His choice to make His home in you!

The Omnipresence of God

The omnipresence of God is something both believers and unbelievers are aware of. The idea that God is "always watching" has been used for either comfort or scare tactics for centuries. In fact, many of the verses I mention below are found in the Old Testament, showing us that people have long been aware that God's presence is everywhere.

Whither shall I go from thy spirit? Or **whither shall I flee** from thy presence? **If I ascend up into heaven**, thou art there: **if I make my bed in hell**, behold, thou art there. If I take the wings of the morning and dwell in the **uttermost parts of the sea**; even there shall thy hand lead me, and thy right hand shall hold me. If I say, surely the darkness shall cover me; even the night shall be light about me. Yea, the darkness hideth not from thee; but the night shineth as the day: **the darkness and the light are both alike to thee.**

Psalm 139:7–12

The psalmist David asked where a person would go to escape the presence of God. Notice his thought process: "Flee" speaks to speed; "heaven" speaks to space; "to hell" speaks of what we understand as the furthest place from God; "the sea" speaks to earthly depth. And "I darkness and the light" covers everywhere else! The rhetorical line of questioning leads to the answer: There is nowhere a person can go to leave God's presence. He is everywhere!

David's son Solomon also had this insight when he wrote the following proverb and when he dedicated the temple in Jerusalem. Here he speaks of God's omnipresence:

The eyes of the LORD are **in every place**, beholding the evil and the good.

> Proverbs 15:3

But will God indeed dwell on the earth? Behold, heaven and the **highest heaven cannot contain You**, how much less this house which I have built!

> 1 Kings 8:27 NASB

From Job to Jeremiah—people of God who were under the old covenant—understood this facet of God's presence.

For **he looks** throughout the whole earth **and sees everything** under the heavens.

> Job 28:24 NLT

For this is what the high and exalted One who lives forever, whose name is Holy, says: "I **dwell in a high and holy place**, and also **with the contrite and lowly of spirit** in order to revive the spirit of the lowly and to revive the heart of the contrite."

> Isaiah 57:15 NASB

> "Am I a God who is near," declares the Lord, "and not a God far off? Can a man hide himself in hiding places so I do not see him?" declares the Lord. "**Do I not fill the heavens and the earth?**" declares the Lord.
>
> Jeremiah 23:23–24 NASB95

The New Testament brings about the gift of the indwelling presence of God—in believers—but His omnipresence is still, well, present.

> God wanted them to look for him and perhaps search all around for him and find him, **though he is not far from any of us**.
>
> Acts 17:27 NCV

Nothing escapes Him; nothing eludes Him. His omnipresence is everywhere and always there. And based on Hebrews 13:8 ("Jesus Christ is the same yesterday, today, and forever"), we know that this presence has never changed. We know that unbelievers do not have the Holy Spirit inside themselves, but we know that they are still surrounded by the omnipresence of God. Whether they are aware of this is up to them.

The Manifest Presence of God

The third facet of God's presence that I want to talk about is the manifest presence. This describes when the presence of God is manifested in a tangible way. And it's something that we can experience in our lives today.

Some people tend to mix this tangible presence with "feeling" something, and then they write it off because they may have heard that we aren't supposed to be feelings driven. The other thing that happens when talking about His manifest presence is that people start to ask if they should be *seeking* this presence and have a tangible "encounter" with Him. To both of these issues, I say just be Jesus driven. Go after Him, and let Him show up however He wants to. He will never disappoint.

Go after Him, and let Him show up however He wants to. He will never disappoint.

Because it is easy to get confused when talking about a presence that you can "feel," let's see what Scripture has to say about God's manifest presence.

> And Cain went out from the presence of the LORD, and dwelt in the land of Nod, on the east of Eden.
>
> Genesis 4:16

When Cain left "the presence of the LORD" after killing Abel, he left God's *manifest* presence. How do we know? Because Cain couldn't leave God's omnipresence. From the time the Spirit of the Lord hovered over the waters at creation (see Gen. 1:2) to now, God's *omni*presence has never left the earth; He is everywhere. And God's *indwelling* presence was not available to humans in the Old Testament because Jesus had not yet opened the way for His Spirit to enter us. Regarding Cain, this manifest presence makes sense because he had grown up understanding that God appeared and spoke to His creation.

Let's look at a few more examples from the Old Testament, when God's presence was manifested to His people and to those who did not follow Him, revealing that He can manifest Himself for any reason and to anyone He chooses.

> And the angel of God, which went before the camp of Israel, removed and went behind them; and the pillar of the cloud went from before their face, and stood behind them: And it came between the camp of the Egyptians and the camp of Israel; and it was a cloud and darkness to them, but it gave light by night to

these: so that the one came not near the other all the night.

Exodus 14:19–20

And Moses and Aaron went into the tabernacle of the congregation, and came out, and blessed the people: and the glory of the LORD appeared unto all the people. And there came a fire out from before the LORD and consumed upon the altar the burnt offering and the fat: which when all the people saw, they shouted, and fell on their faces.

Leviticus 9:23–24

In the first example, the "angel of God" is believed to have been the preincarnate Christ. When the Israelites were trapped between the Egyptian army and the Red Sea, God showed up in a bodily form and moved the cloud of His presence from in front of the Israelites, where He had been leading them, to behind them to block the Egyptians from gaining access to His people. Notice that to the Egyptians, this presence appeared as darkness, but to God's people, He was light.

Then notice in the second example how God continued to manifest His presence during the days of Moses. He continually showed Himself in a visible way as a way to show His support for the leaders He had chosen. In the case of the fire burning up the sacrifice on the altar, note that God's manifest presence was revealed in the form of fire coming from the Lord because He was there *with* them. The fire of His presence did not appear as a distant spectacle coming from the sky.

Now let's look at Daniel 3:24–25 after Nebuchadnezzar had thrown the three Hebrew men in the fiery furnace in an attempt to execute them.

> Then Nebuchadnezzar the king was astonished, and rose up in haste, and spake, and said unto his counselors, Did not we cast three men bound into the midst of the fire? They answered and said unto the king, True, O king. He answered and said, Lo, I see four men loose, walking in the midst of the fire, and they have no hurt; and the form of the fourth is like the Son of God.

Here God's manifest presence was revealed as a person walking around in the fire. Notice that God's presence was seen as a physical being by an ungodly king. And because of God's manifest presence, the Hebrews' bonds were loosed, and they were not affected at all by the fire or the smoke.

Now let's move on to the church age. Even though the indwelling presence of God was now available for believers, we see several instances in the Book of Acts of God manifesting Himself to believers and unbelievers alike. This is proof that God meets people right where they are. If they—or *you*—need a special touch from God, He knows, and He responds.

> And when the day of Pentecost was fully come, they were all with one accord in one place. And suddenly, there came a sound from heaven as of a rushing mighty wind, and it filled all the house where they were sitting. And there appeared unto them cloven tongues like as of fire, and it sat upon each of them. And they were all filled with the Holy Ghost and began to speak with other tongues, as the Spirit gave them utterance.
>
> Acts 2:1–4

On the Day of Pentecost, when the Spirit of God fell on the new believers, His presence was manifested both audibly and visually. The people in the upper room *heard* the sound of a strong wind, it *filled* the room, and then the people *saw* tongues of fire resting on each person's head. Then they began to speak in other tongues once they had been "filled with the Holy Ghost."

Let's see another way God's presence was manifested—this time through a person.

> As a result of the apostles' work, sick people were brought out into the streets on beds and mats so that Peter's shadow might fall across some of them as he went by.
>
> Acts 5:15 NLT

Here we see that the presence of God was so strong with Peter that people were being healed just by being in his literal shadow. The Holy Spirit lingered around Peter to the degree that he didn't even lay hands on them; their healing did not depend on the physical touch of an apostle because God's Spirit was so tangibly present. God's manifest presence is what touched them.

Now let's consider Saul's conversion. Jesus manifested Himself to the "pre-believer" Saul as he was on his way to arrest Christians:

> As he was approaching Damascus on this mission, a light from heaven suddenly shone down around him. He fell to the ground and heard a voice saying to him, "Saul! Saul! Why are you persecuting me?"
>
> "Who are you, lord?" Saul asked.
>
> And the voice replied, "I am Jesus, the one you are persecuting! Now get up and go into the city, and you will be told what you must do."
>
> The men with Saul stood speechless, for they heard the sound of someone's voice but saw no one!
>
> Acts 9:3–7 NLT

Saul (later called Paul) saw a blinding light (the glory of God) and heard a voice speaking distinct words. But the men who traveled with him heard a voice but did not see anyone. This sets up a possible contrast with Saul. By Scripture saying that they saw no one might mean that Saul did see someone. It is probable that Saul saw the manifest presence of Jesus Christ!

What Saul/Paul saw on the road is confirmed in the words of Ananias, the disciple God raised up to pray for Paul. Acts 9:17 says,

> And Ananias went his way, and entered into the house; and putting his hands on him said, Brother Saul, the Lord, even Jesus, that appeared unto thee in the way as thou camest, hath sent me, that thou mightest receive thy sight, and be filled with the Holy Ghost.

These personal encounters with the manifest presence of God were life changing for every individual who experienced Him. Second Corinthians 3:18 says, "But we all, with open face beholding as in a glass the glory of the Lord, are changed into the same image from glory to glory, even as by the Spirit of the Lord.". These are the life-changing encounters that I believe Scripture tells us to expect every day. We are changed from glory to glory by looking on the face of Jesus. How can we be changed from glory to glory if we never see any kind of glory?

We have been unveiled before Him. It has now been made possible to see the glory of the Lord. By coming in contact with Him and beholding Him daily, we will be made more like Him. We can't behold him in this way outside on the streets; we can't do it in church. This beholding must be done personally in our secret place.

Intimacy Activation Prayer

Pray your own words or use what I have here. But let's pray and put off the old mindset and put on the new.

Lord, I ask that you interrupt my day. Holy Spirit, come whenever You like. Just come. I invite you into my car, into my office, into my laundry room, into my kitchen... Interrupt me whenever you like. In the name of Jesus, come.

Take a few minutes to close your eyes. The Lord is going to touch you today. Just whisper this prayer and get lost in Him.

Practice His Presence

We've come to the end of another chapter, and now, it's your turn. Whether you are doing two minutes, five minutes, or an hour, gather your tools, your verse, and your authority over your mind and flesh, and enter into His presence. This time in your prayer closet isn't for prayer-list-type praying. Don't ask Him for anything or even pray for your loved ones. Take yourself and everyone else out of the equation and focus only on Him.

As you continue to practice this, you will begin to recognize that His presence actually fills the space, making it easier to forget about yourself—your needs, your random thoughts, and your flesh. By practicing His presence, you're also making the biblical principle of intimacy a reality in your daily life.

Begin by speaking sweet nothings to Him. Tell Him how much you love Him and what He means to you. Speak words of praise, honor, and worship directly to Him. I've given you the beginnings of prayer to get you started.

Lord, I'm not here to ask You for anything; I'm not here to pray for anyone. I'm not here to read. I'm not even here to think. I'm only here to worship You. Just to look at You, just to put my head on Your chest . . .

Chapter 4

Placing Your Confidence in Jesus

Knowing He Is with You

*I have asked the Lord for one thing this is what I desire! I want to live in the Lord's house all the days of my life, so I can gaze at the splendor of the Lord and contemplate in his temple. He will **surely give me shelter** in the day of danger; he will **hide me in his home**. He will **place me on an inaccessible rocky summit**.*

Psalm 27:4–5 NET

At this point, you have had several sessions of practicing His presence. In addition to your practice at the end of each chapter, I hope you are also taking time throughout your day to quietly worship Him. Even if you can't physically go into your prayer closet, I encourage you still to seek out pockets of time and places during the day to enter your "secret place" with Him. At the end of this chapter, during your practice time, I will be asking you to increase your time. You are probably seeing by now that two minutes doesn't feel like enough anymore.

Seek out pockets of time and places during the day to enter your "secret place" with Him.

In this chapter, I want to address a problem that so many Christians face as they begin to draw near to God regularly. Things are going along well, they feel like they're growing, and their alone time with Him is becoming fuller and more intimate. And then—they hit a wall—or worse, they feel like they have hit nothing, like God isn't even there.

I call these experiences withdraws because, during these times, it feels like God has withdrawn His presence from you or that you are pulling away from Him. You can recognize withdraws when you say or think:

- "I haven't felt the Lord recently."
- "I haven't heard anything from the Holy Spirit lately."
- "I pray all the time, but I get no response."
- "I'm coming to Him, but I leave feeling no joy."
- "It's been days/months/years since [a last experience] with God."

It's common to go through feelings of withdraw every now and then. But the misconceptions are that either God has left us or that we have done something to disappoint Him and separated *ourselves* from Him. Neither of these is true, but the deception seems so real.

This chapter was birthed out of those painful moments in my life when I couldn't "feel" Him. In those times, it was like I was suffocating; it wasn't worth taking my next breath if I felt like He was absent. Life can be hard enough, but it's downright painful without His presence. Life just isn't *life* without Him. It may seem like I am belaboring this description, but I have grown so dependent on His presence that any feeling of withdraw is painful.

I'm sure it is painful for you too. But when we recognize the lie that we are separated from God with the truth that He *never* leaves, we can have a confident dependency on His faithfulness. We can experience this truth and overcome every feeling of withdraw when they come, which is what I want to help you achieve.

The Guarantee of His Presence

In chapter 3, we discussed in-depth the three types of ways God's presence is revealed. The *indwelling presence* of God is everything to us. It is Him living in us through the Person of the Holy Ghost. The *omnipresence* of God is God everywhere, at all times, available for the just and the unjust (see Matt. 5:45). The *manifest presence* is when God shows up in a tangible way; this presence ranges from Jesus on the earth in the flesh to seemingly physical experiences we have with Him one-on-one.

It is this last type, His *manifest presence*, that causes our feelings of "withdraw" when that presence isn't noticeable. Although many of us have been taught that we should not put our hope in the physical, tangible experiences—the goosebumps, the thick air, the hair on our bodies standing up—it's hard not to desire this. Many times and for many of us, it has been in those times that Jesus has shown up and touched us physically. This physical touch, though, is what we're told not to rely on or put our hope and trust in. It's a beautiful thing when He does show up in tangible ways, but this doesn't happen on our timetables.

So, what is guaranteed? When we experience withdraws, what is really happening?

First, let's consider the omnipresence of God and what He promised to the people of the Old Testament.

> There shall not any man be able to stand before thee all the days of thy life: as I was with Moses, so **I will be with thee**: **I will not** fail thee, nor **forsake thee**.
>
> Joshua 1:5
>
> And David said to Solomon his son, Be strong and of good courage, and do it: fear not, nor be dismayed: for the LORD God, even my **God, will be with thee; he**

will not fail thee, **nor forsake thee**, until thou hast finished all the work for the service of the house of the LORD.

1 Chronicles 28:20

God has promised that He would never leave His people. He would always be *with* them—His omnipresence would always be there. So, when we feel like He's not there, like He has withdrawn His presence from us, we know that isn't true. His omnipresence is available everywhere, for everyone, at every time. His word says so.

These two verses reveal the Lord dwelling *with* His people. But man needed to be redeemed before He could dwell *in* His people. The writer of Hebrews sets up this transition from the omnipresence to His *indwelling presence* when he quotes an old covenant verse to new covenant saints:

For he hath said, **I will never leave thee, nor forsake thee**. So that we may boldly say, The Lord is my helper.

Hebrews 13:5–6

Jesus promised this indwelling by His Spirit when He said, "I will ask the Father, and He will give you another Helper, so that He may be with you forever" (John 14:16 NASB).

Forever is forever! Jesus's words assure us of His indwelling—or His presence *in* us—forever, through Holy Spirit. But Holy Spirit's presence in our lives doesn't mean that he just hangs out and is . . . there. His presence has absolute purpose. Look at how His presence is described in Ephesians 1:13–14:

> In whom ye also trusted, after that, ye heard the word of truth, the gospel of your salvation: in whom also after that ye believed, **ye were sealed with that holy Spirit of promise**, which is the earnest of our inheritance until the redemption of the **purchased possession**, unto the praise of his glory.
>
> In Him, you also, when you heard the word of truth, the good news of your salvation, and [as a result] believed in Him, were stamped **with the seal of the promised Holy Spirit** [the One promised by Christ] as owned and protected [by God]. The Spirit is the **guarantee** [the first installment, the pledge, a foretaste] of our inheritance until the redemption of

God's own **[purchased] possession** [His believers], to the praise of His glory. (AMP)

Notice that once you believed "ye were sealed" with Holy Spirit. This "promised Holy Spirit" is the "guarantee" of our inheritance, of everything the Lord has promised us in this life and beyond. It also says that you are "God's own purchased possession." We can think of this as when we buy an item in the store; it now belongs to us. We could essentially slap a sticker on it that says, "Bought and paid for." It's no longer for sale.

That's what God did with us. Jesus bought us with His blood, Holy Spirit moved into us, and the Father placed a seal on us, forever laying claim to His "purchased possession." Remember, though, we're talking about intimacy here. Well, you can't get any more intimate with God than being sealed with His indwelling presence, the Spirit of God Himself.

The King David Dilemma

For years, I've heard mixed teachings about King David and his back-and-forth standing with God. Based on some of David's many psalms, it seems that God was there for him one day but gone the next; David was on a mountaintop, but then he was in a pit; He was anointed of God, but then he begged God not to take His spirit from him. It sounds confusing.

Added to that confusion, many people see David's experiences as something that all Christians should expect (or fear) in their own lives. For example, in Psalm 40:1–3, David wrote:

> I waited patiently for the Lord; and he inclined unto me, and heard my cry. He brought me up also out of an horrible pit, out of the miry clay, and set my feet upon a rock, and established my goings. And he hath put a new song in my mouth, even praise unto our God: many shall see it, and fear, and shall trust in the Lord.

Instead of reading this passage as David's praise of a loving, personal God who rescued him, some New Testament believers read it as something God did *to* David and will probably do to us. I have actually seen a teaching where this Scripture was used to tell us that God Himself will put us in this pit, will make us trudge through the miry clay, and will tell us to just be patient, that our pit experience is for His glory. This teaching ignores the goodness of God and, most importantly, the change of covenants.

What do I mean by the change of covenants? Consider this "King David" lesson offered to Christians. When David was confronted after sinning with Bathsheba and having her husband killed, he called out to God.

> Have mercy upon me, O God, according to thy lovingkindness . . . . Wash me thoroughly from mine iniquity, and cleanse me from my sin. For I acknowledge my transgressions: and my sin is ever before me. . . . Create in me a clean heart, O God; and renew a right spirit within me. **Cast me not away from thy presence**; and **take not thy holy spirit from me.** Restore unto me the joy of thy salvation.
>
> Psalm 51:1–3, 10–12

Under the old covenant, David had a reason to be concerned that God's Spirit would leave him. He saw it happen with King Saul before him. These men weren't immune just because they were kings of Israel. They were still men born under the law and had to live according to it.

But when at the Last Supper, Jesus declared, "This cup is the new covenant in my blood, which is poured out for you" (Luke

22:20 NIV), He introduced this new covenant that was based on His blood. Anyone who believes on Him and His sacrifice enters into this new agreement.

Now let's look at David and his Psalm 51 prayer again. First of all, he lived under the old covenant *before* Jesus had shed His blood and sent Holy Spirit "that He may be with you forever" (John 14:16 NASB). David did not have this seal of the Holy Spirit—he did not have the *indwelling presence* of God. Secondly, David did not have the personal New Testament promise of Jesus that says, "I will never leave thee, nor forsake thee" (Heb. 13:5).

This change of covenants means we need to shift our mindset from doubt and fear of losing God's presence to the hope and joy found in experiencing Him everywhere and every day of our lives. Jesus promised that he would send His Spirit to live in us, would seal us, and would remain with us forever. Is this the truth or not? Forever means *forever!* So why would we think that when we don't "feel" Him in our prayer closets that He has left us?

This change of covenants means we need to shift our mindset from doubt and fear of losing God's presence to the hope and joy found in experiencing Him everywhere and every day of our lives.

When David felt separated from God, there was a valid reason. But when we feel that way, we need to recognize where that feeling comes from and combat it with the promise of His forever presence.

Defeating the Enemy's Tactics

We have an enemy who wants us to think our Father has abandoned us. If the thought of abandonment isn't convincing enough, the enemy at least wants us to think Father has temporarily departed... for a season... until we get our act together. Your feelings of withdraw may be showing up for the first time or for the hundredth time. But make no mistake. This tactic is not new. Encouraging people to question God is the same old scheme. And it's been repeated throughout history and right into our own lives. It all points back to the first deception.

> The serpent was the shrewdest of all the wild animals the Lord God had made. One day he asked the woman, **"Did God really say** you must not eat the fruit from any of the trees in the garden?"
>
> "Of course we may eat fruit from the trees in the garden," **the woman replied.**
>
> Genesis 3:1–2 NLT

"Did God really say?" Just like the serpent whispered the question of doubt to Eve, he whispers the question of doubt to us. It only takes a moment for us humans to step into agreement with a wrong thought, and our minds set off wondering and formulating new ideas and doctrines. Yet those ideas can sound smart, and they can sound like they came from us—or worse, from God.

"The woman replied." After the deceptive thought is planted, we still have a choice. We can entertain it or dismiss it. We can step into agreement with the wrong thought or reject it and come into agreement with God's truth. Eve chose to entertain the serpent's question. We know that because she *replied*. She held a brief but significant conversation with him.

Let's look at the next verse. Eve didn't just reply to the serpent, she went further; she allowed herself to get confused, and then spoke out loud something that wasn't even true.

> "It's only the fruit from the tree in the middle of the garden that we are not allowed to eat. God said, '**You must not** eat it or **even touch it**; if you do, you will die.'"
>
> Genesis 3:3 NLT

But it's not exactly what God said. Genesis 2:16–17 records His words: "You may freely eat the fruit of every tree in the garden—except the tree of the knowledge of good and evil. If you eat its fruit, you are sure to die" (NLT). Eve added the part about not touching it.

Before we put all the blame on Eve, though, we should understand that she had little to no experience fighting deception. And the serpent was especially crafty. But praise God that we have Jesus as our example and the written word as our guide.

Look how Jesus faced the deception of that very same enemy when He was tempted in the wilderness. He was tempted to come into agreement with the devil's deceptive words, but He turned to the word of His Father. For each of the temptations offered to Him, Jesus answered with, "It is written . . ." (Matt. 4:4, 7, 10).

What does that mean for us? When the thoughts come that say, Does God love me? Is God with me? Why hasn't God spoken to me lately? We can go straight to the Word and speak what Jesus spoke: "It is written." These words shut the devil up for Jesus; they can do the same for us. (You can read the whole passage in Matthew 4:1–12.)

These words shut the devil up for Jesus; they can do the same for us.

By approaching deception with the word—reading it, speaking it, meditating on it—you bypass the enemy's twisting of it. But if you entertain the lie and brush the word aside, it's easy to get off track and into all kinds of confusion. I think we all can remember a time when we thought on the wrong thing for a while and watched it grow in our minds. It can get bad! But if you stand firm in the truth . . . well then, "the truth shall make you free" (John 8:32).

Feeling Withdraws

I mentioned earlier in the chapter that I use the term withdraws as opposed to withdrawal to describe the feelings of separation we may feel from time to time. We may feel like God has withdrawn from us or that we've withdrawn from Him. Either way you look at it, the feeling is painful. But it can also be avoided.

Remember God's promise repeated throughout Scripture: He "will not fail thee, nor forsake thee" (Josh. 1:5, 1 Chr. 28:20) and "I will never leave thee, nor forsake thee" (Heb. 13:5).

You may have heard someone say, "Yes, He won't leave you, but you can leave Him." This argument sounds like a twisting of God's word, doesn't it? David explored this idea when he asked, "Whither shall I go from thy spirit? or whither shall I flee from thy presence? If I [go anywhere] behold, thou art there" (Psalm 139:7–8). And Jesus promised that Holy Spirit will "abide with you forever" (John 14:16). If He won't leave us, we cannot leave *Him*. It's just not possible.

This twisting of God's word is a tactic of the enemy that is as old as time. Think of the sneaky conversation thousands of years ago in the garden of Eden. Or the conversation as recently as last week in your own kitchen:

Enemy: You haven't felt God lately.

Us: It's been a while since I've felt much from the Lord.

Enemy: You haven't been in the word enough.

Us: Maybe I haven't been in the word enough lately.

Enemy: If you neglect the Bible, you neglect God.

Us: I've been neglecting Jesus.

We let ourselves entertain these deceptive thoughts, and we're off! We're making assumptions and making promises to get more "disciplined— reading our Bibles, praying, fasting, etc. We think that we're the reason He's not "showing up" in our lives. All the while, the same ever-present, promised presence is just waiting on us to come back into agreement with Him, in agreement with His spoken word, with His written word, and with the seal of the Holy Spirit of promise.

What if we just stop after hearing, "You haven't felt God lately," and we lift our hands? What if we forget about where we are at that moment and just say, "Jesus, I worship you"? Or we sing a little song to Him? We could stop this downward spiral of deceptive thoughts in their tracks.

Now, let's explore some of the reasons I believe people experience these feelings of withdraws.

Abandonment—Feeling #1. The enemy wants you to think your Father has abandoned you. And if not a full abandonment, He has departed at least for a season. Remember the root of this feeling: Did God really say?

Did God say He would never leave you nor forsake you? Did God really say you are sealed with the Holy Spirit? Did God really say that He would send the Comforter who will live with you forever? Did God really say that the Spirit of truth dwells in you, and you know Him?

Yes, yes, yes, and yes! God really did say those things. And just as Jesus did, we can conquer the deception with "It is written!" (To remember where "it is written," see Heb. 13:5; Eph. 1:13; John 14:16–17.)

With this understanding, the questions shift from "Why don't I feel Him?" or "Why don't I sense Him?" or "Where is He?" to the truth, so you can say, "Jesus, I thank You for your promise that You will never leave nor forsake me. I agree with You, Lord. You are ever-present." This helps shift your mind from doubt and fear to agreement with His covenant. And like Eve in the garden and Jesus in the wilderness, the words you speak are what becomes manifest around you.

God's Absence or Pulling Away—Feeling #2. Because we know about the indwelling presence and the omnipresence of God, we know that He is not withdrawing Himself from us. We also know, based on Scripture, that He will never leave us. Yet sometimes people might feel like He is pulling away from them and that He is absent from their lives for a time. Again, these "feelings" may seem real, but they come from a place that is not grounded in truth.

I have an understanding about one of the reasons people might feel this way. Everyone who is born again has a testimony of how they came to know the Lord. The salvation experience is as individual as the person itself. But I would guess that 99 percent of the testimonies I have heard from others involve some sort of "feeling." People tell of sensing a tangible presence, sometimes felt physically on or in them.

This touch is His manifest presence, and it is a very special experience. What happens, though, is that many people who experience this presence base the rest of their experiences off that first one. This means that when the feeling or the touch subsides, the person isn't sure if God has left.

Think of it this way. You probably have a happy memory of being hugged by a loved-one or significant other. Because of that loving touch, when that person isn't around, you can honestly say, "I miss his/her touch." It's the experience of the touch that makes us miss it when it's gone.

In a similar way, the Godhead touched you in a powerful way on day one. I believe that when the sensation of His touch begins to wane, it is an invitation to go deeper with the Lord. It is not Jesus pulling away from us. It is our heightened awareness hearing Him say, "Come back for more food," "Come back and sit with Me." Instead of withdrawing, come closer.

I believe that when the sensation of His touch begins to wane, it is an invitation to go deeper with the Lord.

Tolerance—Feeling #3. This may sound like an odd one, but I think comparing this to something in the natural might make the most sense. Think of something you have taken or done to get more energy: vitamins, medicine, fruit, coffee, or some physical activity. Before you took the product, you had a pretty good understanding of your energy levels. After you changed what you did and increased your energy, you realized that there was a higher level of living or energy at which you could operate. Without this change, you would have gone along at your first energy level, and you wouldn't have known the difference between what was and what could be.

If you have been saved for some time, or you have been experiencing intimacy with Him on a regular basis, at some point, you may have "felt" the presence of the Lord, tangibly or otherwise. Because of that experience, you now have a gauge of feeling or sensation. You know what it's like to feel Him, and you may have forgotten what it was like before you ever sensed anything about Him. You have gotten used to the sensation. I believe it is the tolerance to that feeling that causes people to make statements like:

I don't feel him right now.

I don't feel him anymore.

I don't sense him right now.

I don't sense him anymore.

I haven't heard from him recently.

Becoming Aware of Him

Feeling like God is withdrawing from you or that you are withdrawing from Him are common feelings, but they don't have to be. Feelings of withdraw are rooted in deception. I have found the best way to combat and conquer those feelings of abandonment, absence, and tolerance is to remind ourselves of His faithfulness and become aware of His presence. We know what the word says about where He is and who He is. But sometimes we get lost in our busy lives. And sometimes spending time with Him becomes a line on our to-do lists.

Colossians 3:1–2 tells us,

> If ye then be risen with Christ, **seek those things which are above**, where Christ sitteth on the right hand of God. **Set your affection on things above**, not on things on the earth.

Whew, that sounds good! Set your sights on the realities of heaven—a heart-to heart-encounter with the King of the Universe! This verse shows us it is possible to connect with Jesus any time, no limits, no restrictions.

In later chapters, we will be talking about the importance of meditation (focusing on the word, both living and written) and adoration (turning our hearts to Him). But for now, let's just look at the basic instructions found in Colossians 3: set our minds on the things of God, on spiritual realities. When we practice becoming aware of God's presence at all times, in every place, we *are* setting our affections on Him, and the earthly things around us become less captivating.

Even though we're talking about seeking that which is "above," we're not actually trying to get *to* Him. We know about His indwelling presence. In that same thought, Holy Spirit is not trying to get through the mess of our lives to reach us. Heaven is here now. Heaven is in us. We have all of God that we'll ever need or desire.

John 14:20 says,

At that day ye shall know that I am in my Father, and ye in me, and I in you.

And Colossians 2:9 says,

For in him dwelleth all the fullness of the Godhead bodily.

Jesus doesn't give Himself in portions or pieces. John 1:16 says that "of his fulness," we have received Him. Jesus came in all the fullness of God, and then He poured into us. So we now have His fullness. And nothing less.

I see awareness of Jesus as something very simple—it's cut and dry, with no gray areas: (1) we become more aware of Him, or (2) we let other things take away our awareness of Him.

You have probably heard the illustration of how bankers can recognize counterfeit money. Experts don't go after the countless ways people try to reproduce money; there would be no end to the search for and study of counterfeit money. What they do, then, is study the real deal. They study and handle and get so familiar with the original that it becomes the only form of money they know. They know the feel, the weight, the color, the design of true money, and when a counterfeit comes along, they recognize it.

This counterfeit versus the "real" works in the realm of awareness too. The "real" is the Lord. It is Holy Spirit with you every day, never leaving, always loving, always speaking. The counterfeit is everything else that pulls us from our awareness of His presence. It can be work, finances, sports, TV, and on and on. To be clear, these are not counterfeit things—they are very real in our lives. They also are not inherently bad. This is not a good versus bad issue; it is simply being aware or not being aware. When we study the "counterfeit" presences, we are essentially setting our minds on the things on earth. The good news is that we can learn to become aware of Him in the midst of these other things, and we can learn to not allow them to block our awareness of Him.

Waiting for Two Thousand Years

I was in my living room one day, early in my walk with the Lord. I was worshiping the Lord when suddenly, He showed up. In my living room! It was like nothing I had ever experienced before, and His presence appeared at a greater degree than I had ever been exposed to. It was clearly His manifest presence.

During that experience, I asked Him several questions, but the one I remember most is, "Why is it I don't feel like You're always here?"

His answer was the most powerful reply I had ever heard up to that point. Before then, His voice seemed to be just words on a Bible page. Now He was speaking directly to me. He said, "I've been standing here waiting for you to look at Me to this degree for two thousand years."

Immediately I saw an image of Him standing in front of me; His arms were crossed, and He was tapping his foot on the floor, both impatiently and patiently, yet completely lovingly. In that image, I saw that He was waiting for me—for us—to come to the realization that He's literally standing in front of us, waiting. His presence is not words written on the pages of a book. His presence is a constant reality.

Before we move into the practice portion of this chapter, I want to remind you of the promise Jesus made to His disciples and to us before He physically left the earth. John 14:17:

> Even the Spirit of truth; whom the world cannot receive, because it seeth him not, neither knoweth him: but ye know him; for he dwelleth with you, and shall be in you.
>
> The Helper is the Spirit of truth, whom the world cannot receive, because it does not see Him or know Him; but you know Him because He remains with you and will be in you. (NASB)
>
> The Spirit of Truth, whom the world cannot receive [and take to its heart] because it does not see Him or know Him, but you know Him because He (the Holy Spirit) remains with you continually and will be in you. (AMP)
>
> The Spirit of truth, whom the world is not able to receive, because it doth not behold him, nor know him,

and ye know him, because he doth remain with you, and shall be in you. (YLT)

So when you're feeling a withdraw, don't get roped into believing God has left you. Don't believe that lie—ever. Remember that Holy Spirit is always with you and in You—*always*.

When you're feeling a withdraw, don't get roped into believing God has left you. Don't believe that lie—ever.

Intimacy Activation Prayer

Pray your own words or use what I have here. But let's pray and put off the old mindset and put on the new.

Jesus, I thank You that You gave me a truth to hold on to, a truth that can't be broken by man or principalities. I thank You that You are here. You are with me now. Being across the room wasn't good enough for You. You so desire to be with me that you said Your Spirit would be with me and in me forever. I agree with You, Jesus. You are here.

I felt that this section needed an additional note based on the area you may be struggling with.

If you are one who has been saying, "I haven't heard from the Lord lately," I simply want you to acknowledge the thought in your heart and repent of it. Then pray this (or use your own words):

Lord, I thought You had stopped speaking to me. I'm sorry I got this so wrong. I know you are always speaking. Now, I thank You for a fresh word from Holy Spirit, and I thank you for direction right now.

If you have been saying or thinking, "I haven't felt his touch lately," I want you to also acknowledge this in your heart and repent. And then pray this (or use your own words):

Lord, thank you for constantly being with me and in me and for me. I acknowledge that You're here with me right now, and I thank you for a fresh touch from You. Make Jesus more real to me than ever before! Thank you, Holy Spirit.

Practice His Presence

At the beginning of this chapter, I said that you would be increasing your Practice His Presence time. Well, here we are. Gather what you need to go into your secret place, or just launch right into this time now. But before you get started, if you have been using a timer, then move it up a few minutes. Go from two minutes to five, or from five minutes to six or seven—ten max.

Now, just lift your hands and take a few minutes to praise Him for who He is. Tell Him how much you love Him and what He means to you. Set your affections on Him. It isn't until He is lifted above all things—in your mind and heart—that He can be everything for you. Learn to attach your heart to His. Make it a habit.

Chapter 5

Flourishing with Him

Setting Your Focus on Jesus

The one thing I want from God, the thing I seek most of all, is **the privilege of meditating in his Temple**, *living in his presence every day of my life,* **delighting in his incomparable perfections and glory**. *There I'll be when troubles come. He will hide me. He will set me on a high rock.*

Psalm 27:4–5 TLB

Meditation is something you may have heard of but shied away from because you're not sure what it is. You may have even heard teachings against it. But biblical mediation is nothing to be afraid of. And it's not closing your eyes, clearing your mind, sitting in a certain position, or breathing a certain way. In its simplest sense, meditation is to mutter or to muse (think) about something specific. For the purpose of this discussion, think of meditation as simply putting your focus on Jesus and His word.

We'll talk more about the specifics of what mediation is later in the chapter, along with what this looks like and how to do it. But first, I want to talk about what meditation does for us based on the word of God itself.

The book of Psalms is the longest book in the Bible and reveals an intimacy with God that many Old Testament people never experienced. The topic of meditation is mentioned in the very first psalm when talking about the person who makes right choices about how he spends his time.

> But **his delight is in the law of the LORD**; and in his law doth he meditate day and night. And he shall **be like a tree planted by the rivers of water**, that bringeth forth his fruit in his season; his leaf also shall not wither; and whatsoever he doeth shall prosper.
>
> Psalm 1:2–3

The person this psalmist is describing—probably the psalmist himself—delights in God's law, which refers to God's word. At this time, the New Testament had not been written, so this is clearly the law-based old covenant. Yet, the psalmist so loved the Scriptures that he meditated on them day and night. Notice this was a voluntary act; we can tell because of the two words "delight" and

"and." The law was his *delight*, his joy, *and* (therefore) he thought about the word all the time.

But "day and night" meditation—is it even possible? It sounds difficult—we all have jobs, families, chores, and we may think it's hard to fit meditation into our day. I'm sure the psalmist had these obligations too, but he found the result of meditating on God's word to be worth fitting it into his day . . . and his night. What he's describing is a constant awareness of God's presence. And what was the outcome of all that meditation? The outcome was being "like a tree planted by the rivers of water."

If you have ever boated down a river—or even *seen* a picture of a river—you would have noticed a lot of trees lining the banks. Their branches might hang over the water, and the trees on each side might even meet in the middle. Those trees don't grow to that size by chance. They start out as seedlings and spend year after year drinking from the water. Their roots grow deep, and their trunks grow strong.

The psalmist describes the person who meditates on God's word as being rooted and firmly grounded like a tree growing alongside a river. And not a dry, mucky river either. This tree is planted by the "rivers of water"! Like that tree, with each day (or night) of meditating and soaking up the word, you also will become firmly rooted to the source of living water, a river that cannot be stopped and comes right from the throne of God (see Rev. 22:1).

Here is another look at Psalm 1:2–3:

But his delight is in the law of the LORD; and in his law doth he meditate day and night. And he shall be like a tree planted by the rivers of water, that **bringeth forth his fruit in his season**; his leaf also shall not wither; and whatsoever he doeth shall prosper.

Notice the bold part: "Bringeth forth his fruit in his season." The "his" being referred to is *you*, the person who meditates on God's word, the person who is aware of His presence. Let's rephrase "his fruit in his season" to say, "*your* fruit in *your* season." This tells us that we have a say in the speed at which we are rooted and grounded. It also indicates that we have a say in the speed at which our fruit comes forth!

I am sure you've probably heard that things occur "all in God's good timing" or "God is in control." But we can't ignore this verse that says that you and I can have a part to play as well. Thank you, Jesus!

Now for a third time, Psalm 1:2–3:

But his delight is in the law of the LORD; and in his law doth he meditate day and night. And he shall be like a tree planted by the rivers of water, that bringeth forth his fruit in his season; **his leaf also shall not wither**; and whatsoever he doeth shall prosper.

Another result of this time spent with the Lord is that your "leaf also shall not wither." The verse has already covered "fruit," so what is your "leaf"? The word *leaf* doesn't just mean foliage. The Hebrew word comes from a word that means "ascend, go up, or climb."

So our ascending to the Lord is determined in this place of meditation. For me personally, I find *daily* meditation necessary—even if it is only for fifteen minutes. Like going a day without drinking water, I would feel dried up if I didn't spend time with Him every day.

Our forward and upward progress toward Him will only cause us to grow stronger and more deeply rooted, and it will raise us up to Him faster. And this is for the long term because a "tree planted by the rivers" is a tree that is deeply rooted and grounded. I looked up some synonyms for "long-term" and found a lot: enduring, long-lasting, long-lived, lifelong, abiding, continuing, remaining, surviving, persisting, permanent, deep-rooted, indelible, ingrained, durable, constant and stable.

Notice *deep-rooted* is one of those words. Seeing this list of words was important to me personally because I would spend time with Him day after day, yet I sometimes reached a point when I would say, "Lord, am I getting anywhere with this meditation and adoration?" One day when I asked him that, He spoke to my heart and said, "Your foliage will not wither. Your ascension will not wither. You will continue to ascend to me, and nothing will stop that."

I once watched a video where someone asked evangelist Daniel Kolenda what it was like to be out of communion with the Holy Spirit, even for a moment, and his response was so good: "It's like someone is putting their hand over my mouth, keeping me from breathing."

That's exactly what it is like for me when I'm not practicing meditation daily. Personally, I have experienced those kinds of moments where I have felt as if I was suffocating. When I thought, "Lord, what is this?" I would hear Him say, "You have left me." Now, please know that I don't mean He told me I had lost my salvation. God speaks to each of us differently, and He knew I would understand this as His way of nudging my heart and mind back to Him. It goes back to experiencing those times of withdrawal we talked about in chapter 4. So my "leaving Him" had to do with the fact that I had dropped out of the constant communion and fellowship that He and I had both become accustomed to.

Now, let's wrap up our passage in Psalms:

But his delight is in the law of the LORD; and in his law doth he meditate day and night. And he shall be like a tree planted by the rivers of water, that bringeth forth his fruit in his season; his leaf also shall not wither; and **whatsoever he doeth shall prosper**.

The last part of the verse says, "And whatsoever he doeth shall prosper." This seems almost self-explanatory, but it's so easy to overlook prosperity when it shows up in our own lives. Maybe it's because we have gotten used to prosperity as meaning money or wealth. Prosperity can include this, yes, but it's so much more.

Something happened in my own life that showed this verse in action, but it wasn't until I shared the story with a friend well after the fact that I recognized it as "whatsoever *I* doeth shall prosper." I had just finished my first year of Bible school at the Jacksonville,

FL, extension campus of Charis Bible College. At the time, my good friend Jake had been working at the school and our church for several years and had moved into a position where he worked closely with the then director and our pastor, Danon Winter. His was a sweet position, and I know many people would like to have had it, or at least one like it.

But then Jake told me he felt a call to move to Colorado to help his brother with his business. He had done a lot of preparation to make the move, but he hadn't yet found his replacement. He basically had two positions—school and church—that needed to be filled. I joked, "There must be a line of people waiting to work for the director." "There is," he said back. And then he said, "Do you want it?" Only he wasn't joking.

Charis Bible College has a two-year program. They even have a third-year option for those who want to go further. But, like I said, I had only finished one year up to that point. I still had an intense second year to go through before I would graduate. For that reason, I did not know if I would even be eligible for such a position, especially following someone like Jake, who had done such a good job at it.

Well, the Lord lined everything up—as only He could!—and I was hired two months later. It wasn't until a while later, when I shared this story with a friend, did I see the bigger picture. My friend said, "It sounds like your gift made room for you!" What a wonderful way to put it! She was referring to Proverbs 18:16, but I started seeing it as the final phrase of Psalm 1:3: "Whatsoever he doeth shall prosper."

By that point in my walk of intimacy with Jesus, I had sat with Him so long that I was seeing that promise play out right in front of my eyes. And even though I got busy with my new position, I never slowed down. And though I have also moved on from that position, I still don't intend on slowing down. I continue and *will* continue to sit with Him to the greatest degree possible. And I will continue to let Him elevate me!

Getting that position, telling you about it, and then talking about my times of sitting with the Lord is not about being arrogant. Prospering is just the inevitable result of sitting with Him. Let me encourage you that as you sit with Him, it will happen for you, too!

Increasing Awareness through Active Meditation

So, what is meditation exactly? To meditate comes from the Hebrew word *haga*, and as I mentioned before, it means to mutter or to muse, among other similar words. I think of it as continually mulling over the things of God—on Scriptures, names and titles of the Godhead, personal words from the Lord, God-given visions and dreams, etc. It is a kind of talking to yourself, but it can also be done in your mind. We all understand that it could be very awkward to walk around your workplace or the grocery store or the mall continually or randomly talking to yourself. Most of us avoid—or desperately want to help—people who do that!

To give you an idea of what meditation might look like, I will be sharing what it looks like in *my* life. For you, it might look a little different. It's important for me for mediation to be constant and continual throughout my day. In fact, it is a personal necessity—but not out of legalism. It's out of a burning desire to be connected with Jesus at all times! I continually feel the "pull," and I love it!

For most of this chapter, I discuss meditating on Scripture. If you're busy during the day or new to the Bible or both, this might seem difficult for you—at first. I myself have had times and seasons where I don't feel like I'm pressing in as much as at other times. For example, when I was working at the Bible college, the beginning and end of semesters were always more challenging. It was important to be excellent at my job, but I always wanted to feel like I was in constant contact with Holy Spirit. During those more challenging times, I would ask Holy Spirit to help me, to show me times and places in my schedule where meditation and more focused communion with Him would work best.

You know what? He *always* showed me. Every time I asked, He answered! And He can do the same for you! You don't have to do it alone. Remember, He wants to be with you more than you want to be with Him. Don't let a busy day or any other difficulties deter you from attempting this and seeing how far you can take it.

Remember, He wants to be with you more than you want to be with Him.

I'm going to use Colossians 1:13 as a basis to show you the various ways you can mediate on one Scripture. Although I'll first use the King James Version of the verse, we'll be looking at it in other translations later in the chapter. Verse 12 says, "Giving thanks unto the Father . . ."

. . . who hath delivered us from the power of darkness, and hath translated us into the kingdom of his dear Son.

For me, meditation during the day actually starts the night before. Sometimes when I'm lying in bed, I realize that it's the first time I've slowed down all day. I'm sure you can relate. I go to the Bible app on my phone and read the verse of the day. This makes it easy because there's no searching on my part. I just use the daily verse they give me. Of course, you may have come across a verse in your Bible that you would rather think on—I have too.

Once I have chosen the verse (quickly, no need to second guess yourself), I read it several times and even say it out loud. As Christians, most of us know how important our spoken words are. If your last thought before bed is Scripture, it's likely that you'll wake up thinking about Scripture. Sometimes I wake up with a song in my heart or maybe an image of the Lord in my mind. When I go to bed with a verse, it is very rare that I don't wake up with *something* of Him in my mind. Before my feet even hit the floor in the morning, I'm thinking of Him. What a difference that makes to my day!

Whether you start with your verse at night or in the morning, this is the verse you will be carrying with you and meditating on all day. Meditating on a verse isn't the same as memorizing a verse, although you *will* end up memorizing it. This is an important distinction because some of us don't have experience memorizing things. When I first started doing this, I was new to the Bible, so almost every verse I read was unfamiliar to me. And I just couldn't seem to remember the entire verse. I had to write it down and look at it constantly throughout the day. I thought there was something wrong with me that I couldn't memorize Scripture. But God assured me that there was nothing wrong with me; I just hadn't had enough practice yet.

I got creative and found so many ways to meditate on and eventually memorize the Scriptures. But, again, it's not about collecting memory verses. As you'll see, it's all about how God's word changes us from the inside out when we take the time to wait on him in this way.

It's all about how God's word changes us from the inside out when we take the time to wait on him in this way.

The first thing you can do is write the verse down. Even though I can see the verse on my phone app or in my Bible, writing it down is the first step in solidifying it in my mind. Once I have written it down and have said it a few times, I start breaking it down into sections or phrases. You have probably noticed that your Bible has lots of commas, periods, dashes, and more. Yours may even have two columns of text on each page. Use punctuation, columns, and line spacing to your advantage. These give you easy ways to break up the verses.

Using Colossians 1:13, I would start with a portion of the verse and say it several times: "Who hath delivered us from the power of darkness."

"Who hath delivered us."

"From the power of darkness."

After a while, I might read the whole verse again: "Who hath delivered us from the power of darkness, and hath translated us into the kingdom of his dear Son."

Then, I'll repeat this process, but with an emphasis on a different part of the verse. He has "translated us . . . Translated us into the kingdom of his dear Son . . . Of his dear Son."

This repetition can be a great help for you throughout your day. It's the repetition that builds habit or muscle memory in your mind. The more you do this with this one Scripture, the more you'll find yourself repeating it during the day. You may not even realize you're doing it!

I think of this as an easy process *now*, but don't worry if it doesn't feel easy to you yet. I encourage you to get with Holy Spirit. Ask Him to help you. He knows you better than you know you, and He will show you the process that works best for your personality and your situation. Trust Him with this!

Now I want to look at the whole verse again: "Who hath delivered us from the power of darkness, and hath translated us into the kingdom of his dear Son" (Colossians 1:13). At this point, I have broken this verse down, thought about it, and repeated it word-for-word as it's found in the Bible. But then I start thinking about each section more deeply, and I start to pull little tidbits of information from the verse:

"Who hath delivered us from the power of darkness . . ."

So darkness had a power . . .

A power that we've been delivered from.

We've been rescued from that power.

Thank You, Jesus.

"Who . . . hath translated us into the kingdom of his dear Son."

So it was the Father who has translated us into the kingdom of His dear Son.

Thank You, Father!

"Hath delivered us . . . translated us."

It wasn't enough for You to just deliver us.

It wasn't enough for you to say let Me rescue them.

You took it a step further and translated us.

You changed me and moved me into the kingdom of Your dear Son.

"Into the kingdom of his dear Son."

Into the kingdom of Jesus

Thank you, Lord!

You may know by now that it's hard for me to stop there. Once I get moving with Holy Spirit, I just want to keep going. So this is a condensed version of what I do on a daily basis. But short or long form, I will do it over and over all day. Sometimes I may only get through one section in an hour. That's okay. I have all day and all night with Him!

Repetition Is Helpful

Although you can see the repetitiousness in all this, you may be wondering how to even *get* to the point of repetition if you can't remember the verse. This is a valid concern. We all have days that feel hectic or busier than we're comfortable with. The thought of adding on the discipline of memorizing Scripture just so we can repeat it throughout the day might feel like more than we can take on. But remember, I said that meditation is *not* about memorization. It's about focusing our hearts and minds on Jesus and His word *while* we go about our regular day.

So, how do we remember enough of the verse to meditate on it? First of all, ask Holy Spirit for help! I can't stress this enough. I can give you advice and tips, but the Lord truly knows you. Not only can He show you your best learning style, but He is also the One who brings His word to your remembrance.

I've already said that, for me, meditation starts the night before. Before I go to sleep, I like to come to Him like a child saying my goodnight words to my Dad. I read the verse, and then I will say something like, "Lord, this is the verse that you and I are going to be sharing throughout the day tomorrow." By saying it as definitively as that, as something I *will* be doing, I feel like it means a lot to Him because I'm saying it by faith, and I'm just so excited about the next day! If you adopt this nightly routine, I encourage you to keep things simple and childlike and to not stress about it. Just rest in Him, and know that He will guide you through the process.

When it comes to starting my day with a particular verse, I can use a Bible app or a notes app on my phone, but I've found if I start with physically writing the verse, this helps me with my memorization. And if I read it out loud while I write it (which I usually do), I have used three of my five senses to help get this verse into me.

Writing the verse out is something that I may do several times throughout the day. I may write it on an index card and put it in my wallet. I may put it on a sticky note (or many!) and stick it to my steering wheel, my computer monitor, or whatever may draw my attention throughout the day. Sometimes I've had the chance to write the verse ten or more times during a break at work. If I have the time, I do it.

One note of warning, though. When you're writing out a verse multiple times, be sure to check the original verse once in a while to make sure you're copying it correctly. It can be frustrating to find out at the end of the day that you've been meditating on the wrong wording all day long! (Ask me how I know.)

But what about those Scriptures that you already know by heart? Sure, writing them out could be a good meditative practice. And I do that sometimes. But on busy days, in particular, all I really need is a reminder to think about the verse. In those situations, I'll sometimes just write the verse reference on the back of my hand or somewhere where I'll see it throughout the day. Seeing it there reminds me to take a moment to repeat all or part of the verse.

I want to be clear that how I meditate on Scripture is not the only way to do it. It's also not a legalistic practice for me. It shouldn't be for you, either. This is not a practice for the sake of practice. It is about building awareness of His presence, everywhere, at all times. When I meditate on His word, I feel continually connected to Him. Like you, I get busy, but I've noticed that, in any situation, when I can step back for a moment and take a few seconds to say that day's verse—out loud or to myself, it doesn't matter—

I'm instantly aware of Him. My focus is off my situation and myself and right back on Jesus, which is where my heart belongs.

My focus is off my situation and myself and right back on Jesus, which is where my heart belongs.

Using Different Translations

Before we move on to the next topic, I want to share an additional way I like to meditate on Scripture. It is comparing different versions of the same verse, and it's something I encourage you to try.

I told you that I love reading and studying the Bible. I also listen to a lot of great teachers of the word. I've been spending time daily waiting on Him and meditating on Scripture for a long time now. So, with the amount of Scripture that I have read, heard, or spoken over the years, I've found that I've run into a couple of problems.

The first one is that sometimes a verse or passage becomes so familiar that I'm tempted to think I've exhausted it, that I've gotten everything possible out of it, and there's no more left. The other problem is that maybe I don't fully understand the verse, so it's hard for me to stay with it all day long. When I come against either of those situations, I have learned to ask Holy Spirit for help.

Once again, calling on Him makes me aware of Him and turns my focus to the Author of Scripture. He is able to show me the limitlessness of His word. One of the ways He helped me get past these blocks was to show me the power of comparing Scripture to Scripture. By that I mean comparing different translations of the Bible. Familiarity with certain Bible passages could be more a familiarity with a certain version or translation than with the verse itself.

> **One of the ways He helped me get past these blocks was to show me the power of comparing Scripture to Scripture.**

By now, it's probably obvious how much I enjoy quoting from many translations. My pull toward multiple versions was born out of my meditation time. I have a few copies of the Bible in more than one translation; I read these, but usually I use the Bible app on my phone, which includes a "compare" mode. There are websites and computer software that can do this too. You can also use a hardcopy parallel Bible if you'd like. The only thing with a parallel Bible is that they're usually limited to only two to four versions. (There are some that have eight, but these are not as common. And they're huge and very heavy!)

As a habit, I usually choose about six different versions to look at. I read through all six of them—while always being aware that Holy Spirit is right there with me. Almost immediately, after or while reading, He will start explaining and expounding on the Scriptures I'm reading. He starts dropping stuff into my heart, and it's sometimes these new nuggets of truth that I end up taking with me throughout the day.

I tend to start with the King James Version. Even though it's sometimes considered the most difficult version to understand, it's the one I use most often. My dad told me to always go with the KJV because it is easy to take steps "down," but it's harder to take steps "up." I read that first, and then I progress to the ones that, in my mind, the wording is either more simple (like the New Living Translation) or more descriptive (like the Amplified Bible or Young's Literal Translation).

Here's how I would study this out based on our focus verse: Colossians 1:13.

King James Version (KJV): He has delivered us from the power of darkness and has transferred us into the kingdom of His dear Son.

New American Standard Bible (NASB): For He rescued us from the domain of darkness and transferred us to the kingdom of His beloved Son.

Modern English Version (MEV): He has delivered us from the power of darkness and has transferred us into the kingdom of His dear Son.

New Living Translation (NLT): For he has rescued us from the kingdom of darkness and transferred us into the Kingdom of his dear Son.

Young's Literal Translation (YLT): For He has rescued us and has drawn us to Himself from the dominion of darkness, and has transferred us to the kingdom of His beloved Son.

Amplified Bible, Classic Edition (AMPC): [The Father] has delivered and drawn us to Himself out of the control and the dominion of darkness and has transferred us into the kingdom of the Son of His love.

(The way the Amplified Classic renders this verse reminds me of dancing. He pulls us to Him, face-to-face, hand around the waist; He sweeps us off our feet and dances us across the floor. He takes us completely out of the realm of darkness and someplace else entirely!)

As you begin to do this with your daily verses and repeat them throughout the day, you can see how quickly you'll have said the verse dozens of times, probably before lunch. It is such a powerful thing to do!

I like this process, not just because of the repetition, but because it brings 1 John 2:27 to reality in my life: "But you have received the Holy Spirit, and he lives within you, so you don't need anyone to teach you what is true. For the Spirit teaches you everything you need to know" (NLT). This means that I don't need another man or a woman to teach me what a verse means. I can ask Holy Spirit, and He will show me. He will teach me Scripture *through* Scripture. Although the Lord does use men and women to teach His word, I just love learning directly from Him as much as possible.

If you've been reading this chapter over a few days, I hope you have been able to put some of this into practice. You may already be hearing Holy Spirit speaking to you. You might even have gotten something you've never seen before from Colossians 1:13 or a familiar verse to you. It's what I love about this process—His truth is inexhaustible!

A few pages ago, I told you about times when I have felt a distance from God, almost a suffocating feeling, and He told me that I had "left Him." Well, the following experience I want to share with you might give a good picture of that exchange.

I was sitting in my office one day meditating on a passage of Scripture, and I slipped into a type of vision. I saw Jesus and me at a track race, but it was more of a cartoon version, similar to the story of the tortoise and the hare. (Stay with me here.) It was immediately obvious which one was the turtle and which one was the rabbit when I bolted from Jesus's side and was instantly several yards away. In the process, I had kicked up the dust and left a trail behind me. I was running at top speed, yet I was also moving in slow motion. Then I looked back and saw Jesus still standing right where I had left Him. The look on His face is one I will never forget. It was loving, of course—always loving—but there was also a smirk. A smirk that made me realize that I had literally "left Him in the dust."

Back in my office, I asked the Lord what it all meant. The feeling of leaving Him in the dust, so to speak, was right. He explained how I can go off quoting scripture out of habit, and I get into a kind of default mode. While quoting Scripture is a wonderful habit to have, He showed me that I must not forget who gave the Scriptures. He did. He is the One who breathes life into His word. He showed me—and I now encourage you—to always take a moment to lean into Him. Ask Him which verse or passage to meditate on. Seek His heart on the current situation. And converse with Him.

While quoting Scripture is a wonderful habit to have, He showed me that I must not forget who gave the Scriptures.

It was this vision of the track race that led me to add in the practice of turning my heart to Him through what I call adoration.

Adoration

I hope you have gotten a lot out of meditation so far, but I don't want to jump to the Practice His Presence section until I share with you the powerful combination of meditation *and* adoration.

The *American Heritage Dictionary* defines *adoration* as "the act of worship" and "profound love or regard." Online dictionaries call it "fervent and devoted love" (Dictionary.com) and "deep love, esp. for a person" (Wordsmyth.net). I have also seen the definition, "strong feelings of love or admiration."

Because of the intangible nature of adoration, I also use some quotes to help myself and others understand it:

> "When the habit of inwardly gazing Godward becomes fixed within us, we shall be ushered onto a new level of spiritual life; more in keeping with the promises of God, and the mood of the New Testament. The Triune

God will be our dwelling place even while our feet walk the low road of simple duty here among men."

—A.W. Tozer, from *Pursuit of God*, ch. 7

"Adoration is not a state of mind; it is the preoccupation of the soul with the beauty of the Lord."

—Eric Gilmore, Sonship International

I personally like to say, "Adoration is setting everything aside, fully detaching from everything, and clinging to His heart."

Combing meditation and adoration helps us recognize that we are not just repetitiously saying a verse. Even repetitiously writing out a verse. Habits are good, and repetition is good, but memorization or quoting a passage *x* number of times is not the goal. Adoration is making an actual heart connection with the God of the universe. It is letting your heart "go up"!

Because our hearts are internal—literally and figuratively—it doesn't matter where you are or who is around you. The directing of your heart toward God can be done anywhere. If you are a teacher in front of a group, or you are using public transportation and are surrounded by other travelers, or you are a medical professional rushing through a crowded emergency room, you can still direct your heart to God. In fact, during those crazy times, it's probably more important than ever to let your heart go up to God.

Like the word *adoration*, the phrases "direct your heart" and "let your heart go up" are also abstract. The Lord gave me a great visual to help me understand what adoration can mean in my life. I'm sure you're familiar with what a satellite dish is, but you may not be as familiar with how it works. It is a round metal "dish" whose most basic function is to receive signals from a man-made satellite that orbits the earth. But you don't want it to receive signals from just any satellite (there are a lot up there!). That's why the person who installs it positions the dish to face a certain direction so it will receive the signal only from a specific satellite.

I picture my heart like that satellite dish. I see the act of turning a satellite dish in the right direction as turning my heart away from *self* and toward *Jesus*. We might want to deny it, but most of us are mainly focused on ourselves. And if not ourselves, we get focused on our surroundings. So, when I realize that I need to redirect my heart—that satellite dish—I look down toward my chest, I close my eyes, and I begin to imagine my heart turning from self to Jesus. Once I feel like my heart is fully turned and I've fully got His attention (or rather, He's got mine), that's when I talk to Him.

The conversation can be anything from more meditation on Scripture to worshiping Him to praying in the Holy Ghost. And much of the time, I just listen. The conversation is intimate and sweet. I don't think these conversations would be that way if I didn't take the time for adoration—turning my heart to Him.

Now, I want to get back into Scripture and take a look at a time when King David practiced adoration.

The Amplified Bible, in 1 Chronicles 29:10–13, says:

> Therefore David **blessed** the LORD in the sight of all the assembly and said, "Blessed (praised, adored, and thanked) are You, O LORD God of Israel (Jacob) our father, forever and ever. Yours, O LORD, is the greatness and the power and the glory and the victory and the majesty, indeed everything that is in the heavens and on the earth; Yours is the dominion and kingdom, O LORD, and You exalt Yourself as head over all. Both riches and honor come from You, and You rule over all. In Your hand is power and might; and it is in Your hands to make great and to give strength to everyone. Now therefore, our God, we thank You, and praise Your glorious name."

The word *bless* in this and other passages comes from the Hebrew word *barak*. According to Strong's Concordance, it means "to kneel; by implication to bless God (as an act of adoration)." Within the Strong's definition are also words such as "praise," "congratulate," "salute," "be still," and "thank."

Although Bible teachers and other Christians have understood the word "blessed" in a variety of ways, it is obvious from this context what David is doing. He is lifting up his heart to the Lord. He takes a moment (or rather, many moments; the prayer runs from verses 10–19) to tell the Lord who He is to him. And he does this publicly. He said this prayer out loud to the people gathered, waiting to hear from *David*, their king. But David left himself out of it completely. He fully adored, praised, and blessed the Lord.

This is adoration at its finest. To stop anytime throughout your day and to center your focus on Jesus, and just say, "I worship You, Jesus." No, you don't have to do it out loud in front of a crowd like David did. You can speak as loudly or as quietly as you want, and do it wherever you want. The key to adoration is all about the direction of your heart.

The key to adoration is all about the direction of your heart.

When I first started adoration as a practice, I found it a little difficult to center on Him. Like my early times in the prayer closet, my mind would wander or would be bombarded with things I needed to do. As I've continued to practice it, I have gotten much better at it. And it has changed my life.

Adoration can help us be constantly aware of Him. It keeps our hearts open and ready for Him, both to be ministered to and to minister to Him more fully. And it keeps our ears tuned to His frequency, yes, for a "word" from Him, but for more than that—for unbroken communion and constant communication and fellowship with Him.

There have been times in my walk when I have thought that I'm not getting anywhere with Him or that I'm not getting much out of this process. I have thought, I don't feel very spiritual. I have questioned if I'm just going through pointless repetitions. But He has shown me that even though I haven't always felt like I am moving into Him, it doesn't change the fact that I am! So, personally, I don't always *feel* like I'm getting closer to Him, but in reality, I am becoming more aware of Him and His closeness. By continuing to push through the day through both meditation and, especially, adoration, I experience Him tangibly in my daily life. I believe you will too!

Intimacy Activation Prayer

Pray your own words or use what I have here. But when you do, I want you to put your hand over your heart and say it out loud. Imagine your heart like a satellite dish and turn it toward Him. When you pray, you will be turning away from self and turning *toward* Jesus.

Lord, I am aiming my heart at you. If it turns, just keep resetting me. Don't let my focus turn any other way. I pray You teach me to sit with You in private and in public like the saints of old. I'm all yours, and you're all mine. You want all of me, and I want all of You, Lord. My heart is fixed on You, my Love.

Now don't be afraid to have a quiet moment with Him.

Practice His Presence

It's your turn. In this section, we're going to practice both meditation and adoration because the two go hand-in-hand. You can do this inside or outside your prayer closet and with or without a timer. If you do use a timer, set it for five or ten minutes. This first practice doesn't need to run for hours.

Choose a Scripture that you want to focus on and have it with you, whether on a phone app, in your Bible, or written out on an index card. Speak the verse softly and slowly. Think about each phrase and what it might mean. Break down those phrases and talk through what each word means to you, like we did earlier in this chapter. Do this for a few minutes, and then pause.

Now think about your heart as being that satellite dish turning toward Him, the Giver of the Word. Start speaking the verse again and thank Him for every word, every phrase. At first, this might feel awkward, but pause when you need to, reset yourself, and then repeat the verse again. And then just watch what the Comforter begins in you and hear what He says.

Chapter 6
Meeting Jesus in Different Ways
Experiencing the Power of His Names

*I am pleading with **the Eternal** for this one thing, my soul's desire: to live with Him all of my days—in the shadow of His temple, to behold His beauty and **ponder His ways** in the company of His people. His house is my shelter and secret retreat. It is there I find peace in the midst of storm and turmoil. Safety sits with me in the hiding place of God. **He will set me on a rock, high above the fray**.*

Psalm 27:4–5 VOICE

Have you ever sensed Holy Spirit speak something to your heart, and you understood what He said, yet you couldn't quite put it into words to explain it to someone else? Well, that's what happened to me one day while I was in the presence of Jesus. As I was communing with Him, Holy Spirit put a deep but clear impression in my heart. It was really just one question, but it took me writing it three different ways in my journal to work through it.

The Lord asked me:

- "How many facets of Me do you know?"
- "How many ways have you sought for Me to be revealed to you?"
- "In what ways have I been made a reality to you?"

Through this impression from Holy Ghost, I realized that I had heard and read of many aspects of Jesus, but I felt like only a dozen or so were a reality to me. Some of the other aspects of His character I have only caught glimpses of . . . maybe. And some—well, He's limitless, so there are plenty I don't even know about yet.

Before we move on to discuss another way of building intimacy with Jesus—through worship—I want to talk about some of the innumerable and unmeasurable facets of God's character, of Jesus, the Beautiful! We will do this by exploring some of the names for God that we find throughout Scripture.

You may have already flipped forward a few pages and seen the list of names. And you may recognize many or most of them. You may even call Him by most of them and think that you understand them. I did, too, to some degree. But then I realized There is a big difference between hearing a name or title of Jesus and having that name explode in my heart as revelation straight from him.

There is a big difference between hearing a name or title of Jesus and having that name explode in my heart as revelation straight from him.

I also feel it's a good time to place this chapter here, after the meditation and adoration chapter, because, hopefully, you are already incorporating meditation into your everyday life. Adding to your practice some of the names that describe the Lord can deepen your understanding of who He is and can open you up to some amazing revelations from the King.

So Holy Spirit and I set off together to find some of these new revelations of the Person of Jesus, and He led me to Revelation 4. This chapter speaks of four creatures who circle the throne of the Lord God. They are fully captivated by everything He is. So much so that they cannot bear to look away.

The NLT describes them this way: "In the center and around the throne were four living beings, each **covered with eyes**, front and back" (Rev. 4:6). The next verse goes on to describe each creature as having the head or face of a recognizable being (lion, ox, human, eagle). But then verse 8 mentions their eyes again: "Each of these living beings had six wings, and their wings were covered all over with eyes, inside and out."

If you're like me, you might read the description of these four strange-looking creatures surrounded by the beauty of heaven and wonder why they were made that way. Why so many eyes—and all over their bodies! One reason, I believe, for their bodies to be covered with eyes is to show us that no matter how long one looks, no matter how many eyes one can see with, a person could never capture the complexity, depth, and intensity of all that the Lord God is.

The One who sits on the throne is so mesmerizing that the four creatures cannot look away, and they cannot stop saying, "Holy, holy, holy, LORD God Almighty, which was, and is, and is to come" (Rev. 4:8).

The Author of Life is not forcing them to do this. They are just so arrested and transfixed that it is the only possible result to their existence. And it starts with them fixing their eyes on Him.

I also found the repetition of the word *holy* to be fascinating. Why three times? Of course, these three times are simply a representation of the multiple times they repeat that phrase, forever and ever. But I see this phrasing as another way to show the multiple facets of the Lord God. I believe that each time the creatures cry out, it is because they have just seen something new! It is a continual seeing of more and more aspects of His holiness. Their only response is to worship Him!

Think of your first encounter with Jesus. When you first got saved, you met Him as Savior. Whether at that time or later, if you needed healing in your body, hopefully, you encountered Him as Healer. When you were baptized in water, you met Him as the Great Baptizer. The first time you got an amazing revelation from Scripture, He was manifested as the Word of God to you.

As I walked this out and kept a journal of my encounters with Him, I started observing a pattern. He was revealing Himself to me in different ways. It was like He was continually opening new doors and inviting me to walk through them to get to know Him more, to experience Him in supernatural ways.

An example of a revelation or unveiling of Him occurred in my own life when I saw Him as Elohim during my reading of Genesis 1. The Hebrew name *Elohim* is commonly translated as "God" in the Bible, and it encompasses His all-powerful, infinite, and supreme nature and describes Him as Creator, Sustainer, and more.

I had started over on my Bible reading plan, beginning with Genesis, and was going back and forth between meditation and praying the Scriptures, when I got to verse 21: "And God created great whales, and every living creature that moveth, which the waters brought forth abundantly. . ." I started thinking about how the Creator might have formed the "great whales." The experience I had is hard to put into words; it was like a vision, or it *was* a vision, but it was so full of detail . . . and love. I flowed with Holy Spirit and just watched things unfold.

I watched Him form a pair of whales, yet it was more than a *forming*. He was designing them with such artistic pride! He held each whale in His hands, shaping it and molding it into exactly what He wanted. Everything He did seemed so personal, like how an artist signs a painting, giving it that personal touch. That's what it seemed like He was doing. Once He spoke life into them, He brought them down to the water and let them slip in. The pride and satisfaction I saw in His eyes—the whole experience—made me weep.

This picture of the whales was so vivid, I was curious to see if that particular breed even existed or if it was just a representation for the sake of the vision. I searched the Internet, looking for that whale with the specific grooves and markings I had seen. And there it was! God had shown me a vision of His actual creating of a breed of those "great whales." I was wrecked for days. The amount of pride and pleasure I saw Him hold in His creation is hard to communicate. Every detail mattered, then and now. There were no mistakes, only intentional beauty.

Jesus Revealed through Scripture

So, the name Elohim, as the fourth word in the Bible, was revealing to me. But as I have searched Scripture, Holy Spirit has shown me hundreds of ways that Jesus, too, has been revealed to us. From beginning to end, in every book, chapter, and verse, Jesus can be seen.

Look what Jesus said in John 5:39:

You search the Scriptures because you think that in them you have eternal life; it is these that testify about Me. (NASB)

You search and investigate and pore over the Scriptures diligently, because you suppose and trust that you have eternal life through them. And these [very Scriptures] testify about Me! (AMPC)

You search the Scriptures because you think they give you eternal life. But the Scriptures point to me! (NLT)

When Jesus spoke these words, He suddenly revealed that every word written in Scripture pointed to Him. This means that when we want to see more and more of Jesus revealed, we can search Scripture. He's there—all over! Praise God!

This means that when we want to see more and more of Jesus revealed, we can search Scripture. He's there—all over!

The Practice His Presence section includes a list of over two hundred names of God that I have found during my study of Scripture. Most of them you will recognize as pertaining to Jesus Himself. But as we discussed the Trinity section earlier, we must view these names in light of Jesus's words: "I and the Father are one" (John 10:30 NASB). Of course, considering the infinite nature of God, the list is only a starter. Don't limit yourself to the ones I've listed in this chapter; there are so many more to discover, ones that will become personal to you as God reveals more of Himself to you.

Intimacy Activation Prayer

Pray your own words or use what I have here. But let's pray and put off the old mindset and put on the new.

Elohim, Father, Savior, Beloved Friend, I want to know more of You, more of Your fullness, more of Your glory, more of Your love. Soften my heart to see who You really are. Help me to see you more clearly. Reveal Yourself to me, Lord. I want to know You and only You with every fiber of my being.

Practice His Presence

I developed this list based on the New American Standard Bible. However, because it is also a product of my personal time with the Lord, it has become a mix of translations, and I have been free in the way I've spelled, capitalized, and presented them here.

You might want to simply read through the list the first time, even look up some (or all) of the Scriptures. But then, in your practice of sitting with Him and meditating on His word, spend time on one name specifically. Practice pondering that one name just as you would with a verse you would meditate on for the day or over several days. As you do this, revelation will come. It will usually come gradually, but sometimes it may come as a burst. At some point, Holy Spirit will alter your view of what or Who you thought you knew. He may reveal the dichotomy of the Man who is God, the Servant who is also Master, and the Judge who is also your Savior.

Names of God—222 and Counting

1. Advocate — 1 John 2:1
2. Almighty One — Revelation 11:17
3. Alpha and Omega — Revelation 1:8; 22:13
4. Amen — Revelation 3:14
5. Ancient of Days — Daniel 7:13
6. Apostle of our Confession — Hebrews 3:1
7. Atoning Sacrifice for our Sins — 1 John 2:2
8. Author and Perfecter of Faith — Hebrews 12:2
9. Authority — Matthew 28:18
10. Author of Salvation — Hebrews 2:10
11. Beautiful — Psalms 27:4; 50:2
12. Beginning and End — Revelation 22:13
13. Beloved — Matthew 12:18
14. Beloved Son of God — Matthew 3:17; Colossians 1:13
15. Blessed and Only Ruler — 1 Timothy 6:15
16. Bread that Comes Down from Heaven — John 6:32–35, 48–50
17. Breath of Life — Genesis 2:7
18. Bridegroom — Matthew 9:15; John 3:29
19. Brother — Matthew 12:50
20. Carpenter's Son — Matthew 13:55
21. Champion — Isaiah 19:20

22. Chief Shepherd — 1 Peter 5:4
23. Chiefest of Ten Thousand – Song 5:10
24. Chosen One — Luke 23:35
25. Christ — Matthew 16:20; 1 John 2:22
26. Christ Jesus — Colossians 1:1; 1 Timothy 1:15
27. Christ of God — Luke 9:20
28. Christ the Lord — Luke 2:11
29. Christ who is over all — Romans 9:5
30. Cloud by day and Fire by night — Exodus 14:19–20
31. Consolation of Israel — Luke 2:25
32. Creator — Isaiah 40:28; 1 Peter 4:19
33. Deliverer — Romans 11:26
34. Descendant of David — 2 Timothy 2:8
35. Divine Revealer of the Hearts of Men — 1 Corinthians 4:5
36. Door – John 10:9
37. Door for the sheep — John 10:7
38. Dove from Heaven — 2 Corinthians 3:17
39. Elohim — Genesis 1:1
40. El Roi — Genesis 16:13
41. El Shaddai — Genesis 35:11
42. Eternal God — Deuteronomy 33:27
43. Eternal Life — 1 John 1:2; 5:20
44. Everlasting God — Genesis 21:33; Isaiah 40:28
45. Exact Image of God — Colossians 1:15; 2 Corinthians 4:4

46. Faithful and True — Revelation 3:14; 19:11
47. Faithful One — Revelation 1:5
48. Father's Only Sermon — John 5:37–47
49. First and Last — Revelation 1:17; 2:8
50. Firstborn among Many Brothers — Romans 8:29
51. Firstborn from the Dead — Colossians 1:18; Revelation 1:5
52. Firstborn over All Creation — Colossians 1:15
53. Firstborn Son — Luke 2:7
54. First fruits — 1 Corinthians 15:20
55. Friend — Matthew 11:19; John 15:13
56. Glory — Psalm 24:10
57. God in Flesh — Luke 1:26–38; John 1:1
58. God of Love — 2 Corinthians 13:11
59. God of Peace — Romans 15:33; 2 Thessalonians 3:16
60. God's Own Son — Acts 13:33; Psalm 2:7
61. Good — Mark 10:17; Luke 18:19
62. Good Shepherd — John 10:11, 14
63. Grace — 1 Corinthians 1:4
64. Grain of Wheat — John 12:24
65. Great God and Savior — Titus 2:13
66. Great High Priest — Hebrews 4:14; 7:26
67. Great Shepherd of the Sheep — Hebrews 13:20
68. Head of the Church — Ephesians 4:15; 5:23
69. Healer — Matthew 8:17

70. Heir of All Things — Hebrews 1:2
71. He who Holds the Key of David — Isaiah 22:22; Revelation 3:7
72. He Who Is Coming Amid the Clouds — Revelation 1:7
73. Hidden Manna — Revelation 2:17
74. Hip Breaker — Genesis 32:25
75. Holy and True — Revelation 3:7
76. Holy One — Isaiah 43:15; 1 John 2:20
77. Holy One of God — Mark 1:24
78. Holy Servant — Acts 4:30
79. Hope — 1 Timothy 1:1
80. Hope of Glory — Colossians 1:27
81. Horn of Salvation — Luke 1:69
82. Humble King — Matthew 21:1–11
83. Humble One — Philippians 2:8
84. Husband — 2 Corinthians 11:2
85. I Am — Exodus 3:14; John 8:58
86. Immanuel — Isaiah 7:14; Matthew 1:23
87. Indescribable Gift — 2 Corinthians 9:15
88. Intercessor — Hebrews 7:25
89. Jesus — Matthew 1:21
90. Judge — Acts 10:42; 2 Timothy 4:1, 8
91. Just One — Acts 7:52; 22:14
92. King — Matthew 21:5

93. King Eternal — 1 Timothy 1:17
94. King of Israel — John 1:49
95. King of Kings — 1 Timothy 6:15; Revelation 17:14; 19:16
96. King of Nations — Revelation 15:3
97. King of the Jews — Matthew 2:2; 27:11
98. Lamb — Revelation 13:8
99. Lamb of God — John 1:29
100. Lamb without Blemish — 1 Peter 1:19
101. Last Adam — 1 Corinthians 15:45
102. Leader — Mathew 23:10
103. Life — John 14:6
104. Light of all — John 1:4
105. Light of the World — John 8:12
106. Limitless — Psalm 78:40–43
107. Lion — Hosea 11:10
108. Lion of the Tribe of Judah — Revelation 5:5
109. Living Bread — Matthew 26:26; John 6:51
110. Living One — Revelation 1:18
111. Lord — 1 Corinthians 12:3
112. Lord God — 2 Kings 19:19
113. Lord God Almighty — Revelation 11:17; 16:7; 21:22
114. Lord God of Hosts — Hosea 12:5
115. Lord Jesus — Acts 7:59; 15:11

116. Lord Jesus Christ — Philemon 1:25
117. Lord of Both the Dead and of the Living — Romans 14:9
118. Lord of Glory — 1 Corinthians 2:8
119. Lord of Lords — Psalm 136:3; Revelation 17:14; 19:16
120. Lord of the Sabbath — Luke 6:5
121. Majestic — Exodus 15:11
122. Man from Heaven — 1 Corinthians 15:47
123. Master — Luke 5:5; 8:24; 9:33
124. Mediator of the New Covenant — Hebrews 9:15; 12:24
125. Messiah — John 1:41; 4:25
126. Mighty God — Isaiah 9:6; Jeremiah 32:18
127. Mighty Lord — Psalm 89:8
128. Mighty One — Isaiah 60:16
129. Morning Star — 2 Peter 1:19; Revelation 2:28; 22:16
130. My Lord, My God — John 20:28
131. Name above Every Other Name — Philippians 2:9
132. Nazarene — Matthew 2:23
133. One and Only Son — 1 John 4:9
134. One Lord — Ephesians 4:5
135. One Mediator — 1 Timothy 2:5
136. One Who Sets Free — John 8:36

137. Only Begotten from the Father — John 1:14; 3:16; 2 John v. 3
138. Our Union — 1 Corinthians 6:17
139. Overcomer — Revelation 3:21
140. Peace — Ephesians 2:14
141. Perfect — Hebrews 7:28; Matthew 5:48
142. Perfect Love — 1 John 4:18
143. Power for Salvation — Romans 1:16; Revelation 12:10
144. Power of God — 1 Corinthians 1:24
145. Precious — 1 Peter 2:4
146. Precious (Chief) Cornerstone — 1 Peter 2:6; Psalm 118:22
147. Priest Forever — Hebrews 5:6
148. Prince and Savior — Acts 5:31
149. Prince of Life — Acts 3:15
150. Prince of Peace — Isaiah 9:6
151. Prince of Princes — Daniel 8:25
152. Prophet — Mark 6:4; Acts 3:22
153. Protection — 2 Thessalonians 3:3
154. Provider — John 6:1–14
155. Rabbi — Matthew 26:25
156. Rabboni — John 20:16
157. Radiance of God's Glory — Hebrews 1:3

158. Ransom — 1 Timothy 2:6
159. Redeemer — Job 19:25; Isaiah 59:20
160. Redemption — 1 Corinthians 1:30
161. Rescuer from the Wrath to Come — 1 Thessalonians 1:10
162. Rescuer from This Present Evil Age — Galatians 1:4
163. Resurrection and the Life — John 11:25
164. Righteous Branch — Jeremiah 23:5
165. Righteousness — Jeremiah 23:6; 1 Corinthians 1:30
166. Righteous One — Acts 7:52; 22:14; 1 John 2:1
167. Risen Lord — 1 Corinthians 15:4
168. Rock — Deuteronomy 32:4; 1 Corinthians 10:4
169. Rock of Ages — Isaiah 26:4
170. Root of David — Revelation 5:5; 22:16
171. Root of Jesse — Isaiah 11:10
172. Ruler — Matthew 2:6
173. Ruler of God's Creation — Revelation 3:14
174. Ruler of the Kings of the Earth — Revelation 1:5
175. Sacrifice for Our Sins — 1 John 4:10
176. Sacrificed Passover Lamb — 1 Corinthians 5:7
177. Sanctification — John 17:17; 1 Corinthians 1:30
178. Satisfaction — Psalms 16:11; 22:26; 107:9; John 6:35
179. Savior — Luke 2:11; Titus 1:4; 2 Peter 2:20

180. Savior of the World — John 4:42; 1 John 4:14
181. Second Adam — Romans 5:14; 1 Corinthians 15:47
182. Servant — Matthew 20:28
183. Servant King — Philippians 2:7
184. Servant of the Jews — Romans 15:8
185. Shepherd and Guardian of Our Souls — 1 Peter 2:25
186. Son of Abraham — Matthew 1:1
187. Son of David — Matthew 1:1; Luke 18:39
188. Son of God — Luke 1:35; John 1:49; Hebrews 4:14
189. Son of Joseph — John 1:45
190. Son of Love — John 14:9, 1 John 4:8
191. Son of Man — Matthew 8:20; Luke 19:10; John 5:27
192. Son of Mary — Mark 6:3
193. Son of the Blessed One — Matthew 16:16; Mark 14:61
194. Son of the Most High — Mark 5:7; Luke 1:32
195. Son of the Virgin — Luke 1:34
196. Source of Eternal Salvation — Hebrews 5:9
197. Spiritual drink — 1 Corinthians 10:4
198. Stone the Builders Rejected — Matthew 21:42; Acts 4:11; 1 Peter 2:7
199. Stumbling Stone — 1 Peter 2:8
200. Sunrise — Luke 1:78
201. Supreme Creator Over All — Colossians 1:16

202. Sustainer — John 6; Colossians 1:16–17; Hebrews 1:1–3
203. Teacher — Matthew 8:19; John 11:28
204. Testator of the New Covenant — Hebrews 9:16–17
205. Tabernacle — Hebrews 8:5; 9:11 (also both chapters 8 and 9)
206. The Man — John 19:5
207. The Offering — Romans 8:3
208. The One Who Is, Who Always Was, and Who Is Still to Come — Revelation 1:8
209. The Promise — Luke 24:44
210. True God — 1 John 5:20
211. True Light — John 1:9
212. True Vine — John 15:1
213. Truth — John 1:14; 8:32; 14:6
214. Undefeated Victor — 1 Corinthians 15:55–57; Revelation 19
215. Unique One — Jeremiah 10:6; John 1:18
216. Upright One — Isaiah 26:7
217. Victorious Warrior — Zephaniah 3:17
218. Way — John 14:6
219. Wisdom — 1 Corinthians 1:30
220. Wisdom of God — 1 Corinthians 1:24

221.   Wonderful Counselor — Isaiah 9:6

222.   Word — John 1:1; 1 John 5:7–8; Revelation 19:13

Jesus calls us to *His* heights. He says that we are now one with Him, with who He is (John 17:21). We can do what He does (John 14:12). Although we do not have His unique divine nature as the One and only Son, we are like Him—He made us that way (Eph. 4:24; Col 3:3).

Now that you have read these names and titles of God, take some time and reflect on who you are *now*. Not who you can be *someday*, but who you are *now*—seated in heavenly places with Him (Eph. 2:6; Phil. 3:20) while still here on earth (John 15:19; Heb. 11:13). Wow!

Chapter 7
Experiencing Jesus in Worship
Worship as a Way of Life

Here's the one thing I crave from Yahweh, the one thing I seek above all else: **I want to live with him every moment** *in his house,* **beholding** *the marvelous beauty of Yahweh,* **filled with awe, delighting in** *his glory and grace. I want to contemplate in his temple. In the day of trouble, he will treasure me in his shelter, under the cover of his tent. He will lift me high upon a rock*

Psalm 27:4–5 TPT

Like the words *grace*, *blessed*, and even *church*, the word *worship* can mean different things to different people. Yet, I have found in my own life that worship cannot be emphasized enough. Like Scripture, it is life itself. But there can also be some confusion surrounding what it is exactly. I came up with a list of questions that I have asked of God and studied out over the years and ones that I hope to address in this chapter.

- What does worship look like?
- How do we currently worship?

- Does that worship look like the worship performed in the Bible?
- Is there a better or more "perfect" way to worship God?
- Is He asking us to worship Him for His pleasure or for our own benefit and wellbeing?

In order to answer these questions—as always—we must go to Scripture. It is there where we will get a better understanding of a word that shows up so readily in our church-speak: "Don't be late—praise and worship starts at ten." "I was worshiping in the car on my way to work." "Have you heard the new worship album?" And, with the voice of a radio DJ, "Join us for another commercial-free hour from the city's number one worship station."

I'm not saying there is anything wrong with using this kind of language. It's how we talk, and it's how we understand each other. But for me, in my personal studies, God has shown me that if I don't go back to the word and biblically define certain aspects of Christianity, I will get them wrong or at least be a little off. And with writing this book, it's especially important that I get things right.

To start our discussion, let's look at Romans 1:25:

Who changed the truth of God into a lie, and **worshipped** and served **the creature** more than the Creator, who is blessed for ever. Amen.

Because [by choice] they exchanged the truth of God for a lie, and **worshiped** and served **the creature** rather than the Creator, who is blessed forever! Amen. (AMP)

We see here that it is possible to worship things rather than God. The Amplified Bible even calls it a "choice." But we also know that we *shouldn't* worship anything other than God. So, do you think this warning is for His benefit? Because He *needs* the worship? I don't think so. One who is Love (which He is; see 1 John 4:8) would be secure in who He is. He certainly doesn't need people worshiping Him. I believe He gave worship to us as a tool for us to lift our gaze to Him and change our focus from earthly situations to Him. By focusing on Him, we are now in position to see how heaven views those same situations we just turned away from.

The Greek word translated as "worshiped" in the King James Version above was translated this way only once. It means "to fear, be afraid" and "to honor religiously." It seems that the early Christians in Rome were having a hard time differentiating between the worship that they knew and the worship befitting their Savior. The more common Greek word translated as "worship" means "to revere, to worship." This type of worship means that we don't need to worship the Lord out of fear. But, even now, people have a difficult time differentiating between the religious "practice" of worship and true worship, or adoration and reverence for our Savior.

We are not to be afraid of God or to honor Him religiously. But we are to revere Him, to adore Him, and to honor Him as the highest and most supreme One in existence. When we worship Him in this way, we align ourselves with His life and His work on the earth.

When we worship Him, we align ourselves with His life and His work on the earth.

Revere, worship, adore. Does this describe your times of worship at church? Is this what you do in your car when you worship on the way to work? What about your secret place or alone time with Him—are you worshiping there?

To truly see the depth of the meaning of *worship*, I think it would be good to go back to the first time the word is used in Scripture: Genesis 22:1–5.

> Now it came about after these things, that God tested Abraham, and said to him, "Abraham!" And he said, "Here I am." He said, "Take **now your son, your only son, whom you love,** Isaac, and go to the land of Moriah, and offer him there as a burnt offering on one of the mountains of which I will tell you." So Abraham rose early in the morning and saddled his donkey, and took two of his young men with him and Isaac his son; and he split wood for the burnt offering, and arose and went to the place of which God had told him. On the third day Abraham raised his eyes and saw the place from a distance. Abraham said to his young men, "Stay here with the donkey, and I and the lad will go over there; and we will **worship** and return to you." (NASB95)

The word "worship" in verse 5 means to depress, to bow down, to prostrate oneself. I see it as lowering ourselves as far down as is earthly possible in order to raise up our God and King.

Notice that Abraham knew this word and understood its meaning. His intention was to get down low in worship to God. The other people accompanying him had no idea what Abraham was facing. But he knew the enormous sacrifice he was about to make: his beloved son. When God said, "Take now your son, your only son, whom you love," He revealed the depth of Abraham's affection for his son. I believe that Abraham had shifted his adoration from El Shaddai, the Blesser, to Isaac, the blessing itself.

The same thing can happen with us: We can enthrone in our hearts someone or something other than God, the One who reigns supreme and is to be honored above all. What Abraham had to do in that moment was to choose whom he would worship. Would he magnify the son he had waited so long for and, in turn, disobey God? Or would he return his heart to the Creator, the One who gave Abraham such a beloved son?

Verse 10 clearly reveals Abraham's decision: "And Abraham stretched forth his hand, and took the knife to slay his son" (KJV). In case you don't know the full story, it actually had a happy ending. Abraham did indeed *choose* to obey God, but God never wanted a human sacrifice. The sacrifice He desired was one from the heart.

> But the angel of the LORD called to him from heaven and said, . . . "Do not stretch out your hand against the lad, and do nothing to him; for now I know that you fear God since you have not withheld your son, your only son, from Me.
>
> Genesis 22:11–12 NASB95

So how can we worship now, like Abraham did then? We must turn our hearts to God and recognize His unchanging worth and value. We must appoint Jesus as King over the throne in our hearts. That sounds like a tall order. So, is God asking us to sacrifice our children? Should we abandon our spouses to live in seclusion? Are we supposed to burn all the money we make? No, of course not! As He confirmed with Abraham, God just wants to make sure that He is revered in our hearts above all else. This is what we were fashioned for.

Old Covenant Versus New

As you may notice, Abraham's form of worship is an Old Testament example. But we are living in the New Testament, under our new covenant with Jesus. We need to see what new covenant worship looks like. Let's look at it in comparison with the old.

Example 1: The requirement of a blood sacrifice

Under the old covenant, blood sacrifices were required. These were regular sacrifices the people had to make to cover their sins, declare that they were healed, thank God for His blessings, and more. The animal sacrifices were usually made from the people's own herds (see Leviticus 3, 4, 5, etc.). To the people of the Old Testament, livestock was their top possession, their livelihood; it was everything to them. And God required the most costly animals to become the sacrifice. A perfect ram, bull, or lamb was what He required.

The new covenant was set in motion on the night before Jesus died. At the Last Supper, He broke the bread and took the cup of wine and told His disciples that He was making a new covenant with humanity. The bread was His body, and the wine was His blood, and He was about to give Himself up as a sacrifice for the whole world. Like the sacrifices required in the Old Testament, this New Testament sacrifice was also one of blood. It was also from a perfect "Lamb." But what made this one different is that this was a once-for-all sacrifice. The One to end all sacrifices!

Live a life filled with love, following the example of Christ. He loved us and **offered himself as a sacrifice for us**, a pleasing aroma to God.

> Ephesians 5:2 NLT

For God's will was for us to be made holy by the sacrifice of the body of Jesus Christ, **once for all time**.

> Hebrews 10:10 NLT

It was the precious blood of Christ, **the sinless, spotless Lamb of God**.

> 1 Peter 1:19 NLT

Jesus was sinless and perfect, the Father's costliest possession, yet He gave everything to satisfy the penalty for sin. When I think of this, I'm reminded of the hymn "Jesus, Priceless Treasure," by Johann Franck:

Jesus, priceless Treasure,

Source of purest pleasure,

Truest friend to me.

Long my heart hath panted,

Till it almost fainted,

> Thirsting after Thee.
>
> Thine I am, O spotless Lamb,
>
> I will suffer naught to hide Thee,
>
> Ask for naught beside Thee.

Jesus was sinless and perfect, the Father's costliest possession, yet He gave everything to satisfy the penalty for sin.

Example 2: The availability of God's presence

In the Old Testament, God's presence was conditional. In fact, even though He is and always has been omnipresent, for the people to be *in* and to enjoy His presence was something reserved for miraculous events, anointed leaders, or the pure in heart. Yet, even then, His presence was conditional.

> And the angel of the LORD appeared unto [Moses] in a flame of fire out of the midst of a bush: and . . . God called unto him out of the midst of the bush, and . . . he said, **Draw not nigh hither**: put off thy shoes from off thy feet, for the place whereon thou standest is holy ground.
>
> Exodus 3:2–5

And the LORD said unto Moses, Speak unto Aaron thy brother, **that he come not at all times into the holy place** within the vail before the mercy seat, which is upon the ark; **that he die not**: for I will appear in the cloud upon the mercy seat.

Leviticus 16:2

Who shall ascend into the hill of the LORD? or **who shall stand in his holy place? He that hath clean hands, and a pure heart**; who hath not lifted up his soul unto vanity, nor sworn deceitfully.

Psalm 24:3–4

The Old Testament list could go on. God has always wanted to be with His people unconditionally, but sin stood in the way. Until Jesus. We see in the New Testament that God's presence has now been freely given to us. No amount of works or striving can get us more of Jesus. We simply turn our hearts to Him and have constant Holy Spirit encounters whenever we like.

Example 3: God's chosen place of worship

In the Old Testament, God chose a physical, geographic place in which to dwell and to receive worship. These places included a mountain, a tent, a temple, and even a city.

> And let them make me a sanctuary; that I may dwell among them.
>
> Exodus 25:8
>
> And it came to pass, when the priests were come out of the holy place, that the cloud filled the house of the LORD, so that the priests could not stand to minister because of the cloud: for the glory of the LORD had filled the house of the LORD.
>
> 1 Kings 8:10–11
>
> For the LORD hath chosen Zion; he hath desired it for his habitation.
>
> Psalm 132:13

In the New Testament, He has chosen us—*people*—to be His dwelling place. Each of us is His temple. That means we, our bodies, are literal places of worship!

> Know ye not that ye are the temple of God, and that the Spirit of God dwelleth in you?
>
> 1 Corinthians 3:16

> And the Word was made flesh, and dwelt among us, (and we beheld his glory, the glory as of the only begotten of the Father,) full of grace and truth.
>
> John 1:14

> And, lo, I am with you always, even unto the end of the world. Amen.
>
> Matthew 28:20

Now, let's focus on this temple concept for a minute. No physical structure can contain God's presence. But He chose to enter the physical temple of the Old Testament to be near His people. And provided the people obeyed the laws of worship laid out in Leviticus, they also could enter the temple. Notice that it works both ways: God could enter, and man could enter. But now that the separation between God and man has been eliminated, this temple has become a spiritual one, one where the supernatural can exist. This supernatural truth is that He is in us, but we are also in Him.

Look how Acts 17:28 explains this:

For in him we **live**, and **move**, and **have** our **being**.

For in Him we live and move and exist [that is, in Him we actually have our being]. (AMP)

For in him we live and move about and exist. (NET)

To see how this verse relates to our worship of the Lord, I want to focus on the words in bold: *live, move* and *have* our *being*.

Live. When we spend this time alone with Him in worship, we receive the breath that is necessary to be animated, to *live* as Christians.

Move. When we spend time alone with Him in worship, we receive the "oil" necessary to move. Think of a wheel that squeaks as its center dries out. We, too, can become "squeaky" when we allow ourselves to be offended, when everything seems to bother us, or when we are not kind to others. Think edgy and irritable.

Being. When we spend time alone with Him in worship, we enjoy the river of living waters, the "well of water springing up into everlasting life" (John 4:14). This living water, the well that never runs dry, enables us to remain *being* sons and daughters. By no means am I implying that we could ever lose sonship. I am simply stating that when we return to Him, we receive what it takes to keep returning. In that same chapter of John, Jesus connects worship to these living waters: "God is a Spirit: and they that worship him must worship him in spirit and in truth" (v. 24).

Our worship in the new covenant is great news! We need to do nothing more than turn our hearts to Him and just adore Him. It is simple to worship Him now since we are His temple. We can experience this sweet exchange with the King anytime and anywhere—in our prayer closet, at the grocery store, in our cars, while doing housework or yardwork, while . . . you get the picture.

A Lifestyle of Worship

As you can see, true worship is not simply an entry on your church's service schedule, and it isn't a genre of music. It's a lifestyle. Yes, it can be something you do at a designated time. It is something you can focus and direct. But it is also a way of life. When worship becomes a part of you, you will find that worshiping Him will bring you joy and comfort and can strengthen you when you're weak. It is all-around lifechanging. At least it has been for me.

A while back, I found myself in a very weakened state. I was rather far into an extended fast (something we will be talking about later in this chapter). Through the early days of the fast, I had been worshiping regularly—as often as possible. Things were going well, but one day, I hit a wall. I found myself so weak that I had zero motivation! Even opening my mouth to worship God felt like too much effort. So I didn't.

I was listening to some worship music (for lack of a better word), and after a few songs, I finally started singing a little. But it didn't last long. I just kind of shut down again. This was so unlike me, and I was discouraged and disappointed in myself that I couldn't even sing a simple song to worship Jesus. I guess I started whining—in my heart; I wasn't even motivated enough to whine out loud.

Then, suddenly, I felt the sweet, sweet presence of Jesus come over me. Immediately, I turned my heart toward Him and gave Him my full attention. He spoke so kindly to me; He said, "I never asked for your words. I've only ever wanted your heart."

I was undone to the greatest degree! I know and have told others the same thing, that our words mean little. What He really wants is our hearts. But in my weakened physical state, I had let the truth slip. His reminder to me was powerful and forever memorable.

For the remainder of this chapter, we will be exploring various ways that you can incorporate worship into your life until it becomes your own lifestyle. This is not a to-do list where you need to check off every item before you can be complete. We are already "complete in Him" (Col. 2:10). These are various things for you to explore worship, and in partnership with Holy Spirit, you will find the sweet spot in your intimacy with Him.

Worship and Word

I think it's safe to say that looking into the word or reading the Bible is like looking into a mirror to see and hear who we are (see 1 Cor. 13:12). I believe the reason this isn't more ingrained in us is because we don't spend enough time in worship. If I could say it another way—the reason we don't become more of what the word says we are is because we don't get alone and worship enough. *Enough*, not in a legalistic sense, but it's the amount needed for *us* to grow in the truth of who we are.

Worship is our encounters with the Lord where He is able to make what we have read a reality in our daily lives, where we are not just reading about our God, but we are actually having a heart-to-heart encounter with Him. The more we read, and then the more we worship, the more we encounter Him; it's a blessed heart exchange! And the more often the exchange, the more fuel on the fire of a vibrant relationship with Jesus.

Once that fire is rolling, over weeks and months, worship becomes an issue of "throwing another log on the fire." See, as we encounter Him through worship and the word, the word leads us to Him, which creates or enhances an environment of us continually turning to His word and worshiping Him out of admiration for who He is.

So, what does this look like? Most of you reading this book probably do this method to some degree already. For example, say I'm reading in the book of Luke, and Holy Spirit highlights a word or phrase or even a whole passage, then I just sit there with Him and mull over it. I ask Him questions about it and engage in conversation with Him over it. In fact, I literally do engage in conversation with Him; I find that verbal, out-loud conversations are best for me.

Now, say I've been mulling over a passage, but I'm not getting anywhere; I feel like I've hit a roadblock. Then instead of going back to that passage and trying to keep figuring it out, I start worshiping Him. I might worship sitting down or standing up or while pacing the floor. The way to worship is personal to each person. The encounters occur between you and Holy Spirit. No one else.

The way to worship is personal to each person. The encounters occur between you and Holy Spirit. No one else.

One thing I want to stress about worship is that it is *not* difficult. It is important not to overthink it. Let's look at Luke to see how simple it can be to worship God.

And He said to them, "When you pray, say: 'Father, hallowed be Your name. Your kingdom come.'"

Luke 11:2 NASB

I mentioned that when I hit a roadblock with a certain Scripture, that's when I start worshiping Him. I take steps that almost mimic my times of meditating on the word, and I let Him open my understanding.

My first look at the Scripture—"Say." When I first read this verse during a time of worship, the word that popped out to me was "say." I'm sure by now you know why—we must talk to Him like He is real. Because He is.

Then, after seeing that word, I started asking some questions: Jesus, why did You tell us to "say"? How is that important? Is it important for You or for me? What does that look like? Does it touch the Father's heart when I speak to Him? What does touching the Father's heart look like?

In this questioning, He speaks to my heart and reveals things to me. I don't usually ask so many questions at this point in my life. Our relationship has come to a place where He and I just converse, and it's like my questions are answered before I even ask, naturally.

My second look at the Scripture—"Father." Just that one word, "Father," can lead us down many paths; I know it can me. So I wanted to know, what is just one thing Jesus is saying here? He showed me that, in the Old Testament, people called Him *Lord, Elohim, Adonai*. But now, He wants us to see Him as a Father. He asks us to call Him *Father, Abba, Dad.* To the Jews, this was huge! They had always seen Him as a Godfather, one to be feared, but Jesus said they could now see Him as a *Father*, a Dad.

I'm using this verse as a real example of how I meditated on it during a time of worship. But the process is one I have gone through many times for many different passages. After mulling this verse over for thirty minutes or so, I got kind of stuck. I thought that maybe Holy Spirit was done with this one, or I had reached the end of what I could get out of this verse. At times I've been tempted to just move on to something else or at least move on in my reading until something else strikes me. But I have found that when I refuse to move on, my determination is always worth it. My refusal to move on was and is not out of rebellion but, rather, out of the knowledge that He is a never-ending ocean, a well that never runs dry! In this case (and others), I worshiped for a few minutes more when suddenly, I saw something else.

My third look at the Scripture—Adoption. Focusing on the word "Father" brought another Scripture to mind: "Ye have received the Spirit of adoption, whereby we cry, Abba, Father" (Rom. 8:15). Now, to me, that word shouts adoption! Jesus is saying that you're adopted! God is trying to father you. Some of you may have grown up with a messed up father or no father at all, and some may have been part of a religious church that portrayed God as a dictator or control freak, both of which skewed your view of Him as a loving Father. Well, adoption into His family undoes every negative parental situation. God is loving, merciful, kind, and every good thing we can think of. He is constantly pursuing us, always speaking, and always available. What a good Dad!

I'd like for you to just stop and focus on this verse (or any verse) a moment longer. Let's not rush. I encourage you also to return to it another day. I have found that when I go back to the same verse, the Lord continues to show me more. Sometimes it's a deeper look into the same topic, and sometimes it's a completely different aspect of the verse. Even use a timer so you can commit to staying put for a length of time. This whole process can help in several ways:

1. It forces you to stay where you are and not move on. Jesus isn't antsy or eager to move on. We are. Jesus could hang out with you all day.
2. It crushes the mind and flesh simultaneously. When you turn the time over to Him, your flesh may go wild. This process

forces your flesh to submit to your spirit, which is already perfectly submitted to the Lord.

3. It gives Holy Spirit time to speak to you. Often, we accidentally rush past something that He has been trying to speak to us for days, months, or even years. Sitting here in this manner allows Him to speak and opens you up to listen more attentively.
4. It gives God time to work that "thing" out in us. That *thing* is whatever He is wanting to do in us. Often, we make the mistake of getting a revelation but never letting it settle in us. But He wants what He shows us to become so much a part of us that we can never "unsee" it.

Worship and Proclamation

Have you ever heard a minister say, "You get Him as you preach Him" or "He manifests as the message"? I have. What those ministers have figured out is that Jesus reveals Himself as the topic of the sermon. If a person preaches healing, Jesus shows up as Healer, and people get healed. If they preach salvation, He shows up as Savior, and people get saved. So, when we worship Him and proclaim Him as undefeated Victor, then He shows up in our lives as the undefeated Victor! He loves to manifest in the ways we speak about Him. If you proclaim Him as your Healer, then it's that side of Him that you will experience.

This practice is what I call worship and proclamation. You are proclaiming Him as what you need, desire, or just how you want to experience Him.

Remember that "abbreviated" list of 222 names of God in the last chapter? There's a reason He has so many identifiers. He is not confused about Himself. He knows who He is. He is "I AM" (Ex. 3:14). He is everything! And He can be everything to you.

Right now, take a moment and turn back to that list in the previous chapter. Choose a name that stands out to you. You may feel a prompting from Holy Spirit toward a specific name. But don't worry if you don't. Just pick one that means something to you. Now close your eyes, turn your heart to Him, and speak out that name slowly and softly. Thank Him for being *that* to you. Take all the time you need.

Incorporate that name and the accompanying Scripture(s) into your mediation or prayer closet time; it can help you stay focused and on track. Remember that His word leads you to Him. Think on the passage and speak this name over the next several days and watch Jesus show up! Just make sure you stick around long enough to meet Him!

Remember that His word leads you to Him.

Worship and Waiting

A second way to practice worship is through worship and waiting. Worship and waiting imply that when you worship, you should always take a certain amount of time to quietly wait on the Lord. This is why worshiping with music is common. The slower rhythm and quieter volume help us slow down physically. And the repetition of the lyrics helps our mind to rest.

I don't mean that you and I are "waiting" on Him in the sense that His work is not complete. We wait on Him as a way for us to crush our "Adamic" tendencies and magnify Jesus in us. I used the word *crushed* for a reason. We are not trying to suppress or hide a carnal or unregenerate nature. King Jesus came and crushed that thing for us already. What we do is turn to Him, spend time with Him daily, and we come back into line with Him. We realize, then, that this nature has already been crushed, and we are each a new creation (see 2 Cor. 5:17).

I believe that many people stop short of having a heavenly encounter because they are satisfied with surface-level theology. Let's be a people who go deeper. Let's not stop short of what Jesus wants to do in us or what Holy Spirit wants to show us. There is no set physical position or length of time, or any other requirements for worshiping the Lord. I've worshiped with music that was instrumental or had singing that was on video or audio only. But I've also worshiped with nothing at all. I've moved from standing to kneeling, to sitting, to lying down. I've worshiped with a timer going. And I've completely ignored the clock. The key is simply giving that time fully to the Lord. This is not the time for chores or other daily tasks, like you might do when you're meditating on Scripture. Worship time is time specifically set aside for Him.

The key is simply giving that time fully to the Lord. Worship time is time specifically set aside for Him.

Worship and Fasting

I love fasting! That statement might not be something that comes out of most Christians' mouths. But I urge you not to skip this section. Hear me out as I tell you why I love it and how it can elevate your own worship time.

First of all, we can't discuss fasting without discussing our own personal alone time with the Lord. There is no point in fasting if we're not intimate with Him. Without this intimacy, fasting just becomes another religious act, and an unpleasant one at that. Intimacy involves continually turning our hearts to Him, loving Him, and letting Him love us every moment of the day.

We are now more than halfway through this book, but I feel I need to stress that if you are not getting alone with the Bridegroom if you are not having heart encounters with Him, put this book down and go! Go be alone with Him. When I teach a group of people, I am not usually bossy or demanding. I don't usually tell them what to do. But these heart encounters and this intimacy are necessities in our lives. It is vital to my life and to yours! Go and get alone with the Bridegroom. Have a heart encounter with King Jesus right now.

Now, let's discuss what fasting is and why we do it. Fasting is abstaining from food (the physical realm) to focus more on Jesus (the spiritual realm). It's taking the thought of food and the act of eating and setting them aside to spend more time with the Lord. Many people think that fasting means giving up whatever they feel is necessary: food, sugar, television, social media, etc. I believe that giving up anything other than food is actually a discipline, not a fast. However, because you are growing in intimacy with Jesus, what you "fast" is solely between the two of you. What you two decide is personal; I won't get in the way.

For some people, giving up food entirely or giving up food *and* water may not work for their health situation. In the following pages, I will be sharing what Scripture says and sharing my own personal experiences only. You do with it as you will.

So, fasting, for the purposes of this chapter, is giving up food and food-related practices. But why do we do it? We fast because we are hungry for more of Him. We want to make *Him* our bread and partake of Him. We do this, not because we don't already have all of Him, but because we want to reveal that we *do* have all of Him. We think of food as being our sustenance, but it is not really enough to sustain us. Only He can do that. This is what Jesus meant when He said, "Man shall not live by bread alone, but by every word that proceedeth out of the mouth of God" (Matt. 4:4).

Fasting is mentioned dozens of times throughout the Bible—both in the Old and New Testaments. It is mentioned over 70 times in the King James Version, over 80 in the New Living Translation, and over 140 times in the Amplified Classic Bible. In these mentions, there are also several types of fasts, from the extreme of an absolute fast to a water-only fast, to a juice fast, to the fast practiced by Daniel—only fruits and vegetables.

An absolute fast means abstaining from both food and water and can be found in Jonah 3:7 when the king of Nineveh declared a fast for his city. The Bible does not state how long the people fasted, but some traditions say it may have been up to three days.

A water-only fast is abstaining from food, but water can still be consumed. An example of this can be found in Matthew chapter 4 when Jesus was led by the Spirit into the wilderness, and He fasted for forty days. Note that this is a long time, and Jesus did it only as he was led by Holy Spirit.

The way Daniel and his friends fasted can be found in two different places in the Book of Daniel. Daniel said, "Please test us for ten days on a diet of vegetables and water" (1:12 NLT), and later he wrote, "All that time I had eaten no rich food. No meat or wine crossed my lips, and I used no fragrant lotions until those three weeks had passed" (10:3 NLT). The Daniel fast we hear about today is somewhat flexible and left up to interpretation. However, it is usually understood as abstaining from everything except fruits, vegetables, and water.

To go any further in our discussion of fasting, we're going to need to address the first sin. Why the first sin? Well, let's turn there and see.

Genesis 3:1–6 NLT:

The serpent was the shrewdest of all the wild animals the Lord God had made. One day he asked the woman, "Did God really say you must not eat the fruit from any of the trees in the garden?"

"Of course we may eat fruit from the trees in the garden," the woman replied. 3 "It's only the fruit from the tree in the middle of the garden that we are not allowed to eat. God said, 'You must not eat it or even touch it; if you do, you will die.'"

"You won't die!" the serpent replied to the woman. "God knows that your eyes will be opened as soon as you eat it, and you will be like God, knowing both good and evil."

The woman was convinced. She saw that the tree was beautiful and its fruit looked delicious, and she wanted the wisdom it would give her. So she took some of the fruit and ate it. Then she gave some to her husband, who was with her, and he ate it, too.

It is interesting to see that the first sin involved eating a certain food. Of course, eating food is not a sin in itself. But eating of this tree was the only thing God had commanded Adam and Eve to *not* do. They were free to roam the garden (which was their entire world), eat of any other tree, hang out with God—you name it—but the one thing that the devil could actually tempt them with was a tasty piece of fruit.

In that one act of not resisting, the first man and woman gave up intimacy with God. We sometimes say that they lost their relationship with Him. But the word *relationship* has a very surface-level sound; it lacks the depth of the sweet, unhindered love exchange with the Lord Almighty that man gave up.

If mankind could *lose* intimacy by eating food that was forbidden, what can we *gain* by abstaining from it? That's right, intimacy. We know that Jesus's death and resurrection are what bought us back and opened the door to intimacy. This unhindered love exchange is not automatic. As you know by now, intimacy is built; it's grown. Jesus made a way. Now we must walk in it. So, by separating ourselves from the thing that caused the fall, we can turn toward the very Person Adam and Eve had turned away from. We can put food down temporarily to lift God up and focus on Him.

This unhindered love exchange is not automatic. As you know by now, intimacy is built; it's grown. Jesus made a way.

Fasting is addressed in various places in the Old Testament, but I want to jump to the Gospels and talk about how Jesus referenced fasting when he was confronted by others.

> Then the disciples of John came to Him, asking, "Why do we and the Pharisees fast, but Your disciples do not fast?" And Jesus said to them, "The attendants of the bridegroom cannot mourn as long as the bridegroom is with them, can they? But the days will come when the bridegroom is taken away from them, **and then they will fast**.
>
> Matthew 9:14–15 NASB95

Maybe John's disciples—and the Pharisees—were grouchy fasters. They adhered to the religious law, even when they didn't understand the purpose. And they were hungry. They must have seen Jesus and His disciples eating and enjoying themselves and just had to ask about it.

Jesus explained that they were eating (and enjoying life) because the bridegroom (Himself) was with them right now. I see it this way—the bread of intimacy was being fed to them, right then. They didn't need intimacy in any other way, and they didn't need to fast because intimacy wasn't absent from them. Jesus, the Bridegroom, Intimacy Itself, was present with them.

The same incident is described in Mark.

> Jesus replied, "Do wedding guests fast while celebrating with the groom? **Of course not.** They can't fast while the groom is with them.
>
> Mark 2:19 NLT

> Jesus answered them, Can the wedding guests fast (abstain from food and drink) while the bridegroom is with them? As long as they have the bridegroom with them, they **cannot** fast.
>
> Mark 2:19 AMPC

Jesus saw this as an absurd question. His "of course not" is His way of saying, "Why are you even asking me this question? It doesn't make sense that you would even ask this because *I* am the Bread of Life. I am with them. They are feeding on Me and partaking of Me." The Amplified above (and other translations) says, "They cannot fast." Why? Because the person of Jesus Christ was in their presence at that very moment.

I want to visit Luke 5 to expand on what Jesus said during this event.

> And Jesus said to them, "You cannot make the attendants of the bridegroom fast while the bridegroom is with them, can you? But the days will come, and when the bridegroom is taken away from them, then they will fast in those days." And He was also telling them a parable: "No one tears a piece of cloth from a new garment and puts it on an old garment; otherwise he will both tear the new, and the piece from the new will not match the old. And no one puts new wine into old wineskins; otherwise, the new wine will burst the skins, and it will be spilled out, and the skins will be ruined. But new wine must be put into fresh wineskins.

And no one, after drinking old wine, wishes for new; for he says, 'The old is good enough.'"

Luke 5:34–39 NASB95

In all three of these Gospel accounts, we see Jesus using the same terminology: "the bridegroom." Isn't it curious that Jesus would use this word? The bride and bridegroom relationship shouts intimacy. It shouts, "alone time." So, again, there was no need for the disciples to fast while Jesus was with them. They were already enjoying intimacy with the Lord.

Now notice the shift to Jesus talking about garments and wineskins. Jesus said, "No one tears a piece of cloth from a new garment and puts it on an old garment . . . the piece from the new will not match the old." How does this relate to intimacy with the Bridegroom? Think about it. Jesus did not leave the glory of heaven to become a "patch" on an old garment or dead spirit. He came to become one "fabric" with His creation, to make us new beings.

The same goes for the wineskins. Jesus said, "And no one puts new wine into old wineskins; otherwise, the new wine will burst the skins, and it will be spilled out, and the skins will be ruined." He doesn't leave us hanging on this negative "thou shalt not" note, but He finishes out the illustration with: "New wine must be put into fresh [new] wineskins." The only way for Jesus to have an intimate relationship with us is to first make us compatible with Him by making us new. The old won't work. Essentially, Jesus is saying, "The only way for Me to be intimate with you in the way I want to be is to die, rise again, and put My life in your new life. *Then* I can pour myself into you."

When we reach out to Him for salvation, He makes us new. New garment. New wineskin. We become one with Him, and we now have the freedom of unhindered fellowship with Him whenever we like. And because we are born again, we can receive the gift of Holy Spirit—the new wine—who lives perfectly and powerfully inside this new wineskin.

Now that we are new, and we are God's children, some people think that anything that happened in the Old Testament is, well, "old" and no longer applies. It is true that we need to read the Old Testament in light of the New and of Jesus's finished work. But both Paul and Peter spoke of looking at Old Testament events as learning experiences or warnings.

> Now these things **happened to them as an example**, and they were **written for our instruction**, upon whom the ends of the ages have come.
>
> 1 Corinthians 10:11 NASB

> For if God did not spare angels when they sinned, . . . and did not spare the ancient world, but protected Noah, . . . and if He condemned the cities of Sodom and Gomorrah to destruction . . . **having made them an example** of what is coming for the ungodly; and if He rescued righteous Lot, . . . **then the Lord knows how to rescue the godly** from a trial.
>
> 2 Peter 2:6–9 NASB

How do these Scriptures relate to fasting? First of all, remember how Jesus answered John's disciples in Matthew 9:15: "But the days will come when the bridegroom is taken away from them, and **then they will fast**." This fasting would take place *after* Jesus made a new covenant and went to the cross. They would become new covenant saints, yet Jesus still expected them to fast.

See, I believe that fasting *reveals* His fullness in our lives. His fullness is in us all the time, but we are not walking it out completely, and it's not fully showing up in the church. What is the missing element? Fasting. We can find out who we are in Him by making the Bread of Life our "bread"—our food. Fasting unveils Jesus, which is why He said that His disciples would fast *after* the cross.

I've talked about how much I like to ask the Lord questions. Knowing the *purpose* behind something is very important to me. This goes for fasting too. Look at what the prophet Joel said as he gave God's message, calling on 'His people to turn to Him:

> Turn to me now, while there is time. Give me your hearts. Come with **fasting**, weeping, and mourning.
>
> Joel 2:12 NLT

It is important to note that the verse in Joel that calls on people to fast is in the same chapter where Joel prophesied the coming of Holy Spirit (see 2:28–29)—a direct reference to the New Testament and quoted by Peter in Acts 2. But the thing that is most important in Joel 2:12 is the *purpose* of the fast, which can be found more clearly in the Amplified Classic:

> Therefore also now, says the Lord, turn and keep on coming to Me with all your heart, with fasting, with weeping, and with mourning [**until every hindrance is removed and the broken fellowship is restored**].

In the last few chapters, I have used the phrase "turn to Him" or something similar. But turning to God can seem like an abstract concept. How do we turn to Him? And considering the verse above, how do you do it "with all your heart"? The answer is found immediately after: "With fasting." For the born-again person, this turning to Him does not mean salvation. That has already been done. Fasting is done so that "every hindrance is removed and the broken fellowship is restored." In a word—Intimacy!

As we make our way in this world, we encounter a lot of ungodly things. We may even act ungodly at times. We have not lost our salvation or our "newness," but we can get weighed down. Life-stuff can stick to us. I think of it like a clogged drainpipe. When you have a slow-moving or completely clogged drain, you go to the store and buy a bottle of drain cleaner. You pour it down the drain, let it sit for a while, and let it do its work. And with enough time and enough "power," your pipe is cleared!

Fasting is like that. It cleans you out. It makes you fully open and accessible to Him. Remember that Jesus knew we would have His fullness after the cross, yet He still expected us to fast. So, a new covenant believer, one who is a new creation, one who has Holy Spirit living inside, must learn from Joel's prophecy and Jesus's teaching. Making fasting part of your worship of Him increases intimacy with Him. It helps you make Him your only One, all you can see. All other desires just fall off.

Worship in the Spirit

Praying in the Spirit. Speaking in other tongues. However you want to refer to it, churches have split, and entire denominations have sprung up over this one doctrinal issue. The fact that I am addressing it as an aspect of worship will clue you in on which side I stand. I love God's word, and in reading the Bible, I have clearly seen this facet of the Christian experience. For this section, then, I am going to assume you have experienced the baptism of the Holy Spirit with the evidence of speaking in tongues. Even if you don't speak in tongues often or haven't since the day you received, this section is still for you.

Praying in tongues is a vital part of your worship time. Please don't neglect it. You know that I take my time with the Lord very seriously. I have spent hours and days over several years just sitting with him, growing in intimacy with Him. Yet, when it came to using my prayer language in worship, I found the practice uncomfortable. I could fast for days, sit in silence for hours, meditate on Scripture, and sing worship songs, yet I found myself fumbling around when I tried to worship in tongues. I had heard that it was a great way to direct my worship toward Him, but I hadn't really practiced it.

The fact that I'm talking about it now, however, means that I finally found my way through my uncertainty. It is now a regular part of my worship. How did I get used to it? By singing! Yes, singing in tongues, quietly, alone (with Him), and fumbling at first.

I chose a song that was short (it had three lines—sixteen words total) and one I had memorized because I had sung it often in church. I sang it a few times through and allowed myself to rest and enter into worship. Once I felt comfortable worshiping with the song, I slowed it down and switched over to tongues while still keeping the melody.

This simple method is the one that Holy Spirit helped me implement. Ask Him to show you the best way for you to get past your discomfort. Up to that time, I had been praying in the Spirit for a while, but singing in the Spirit—it was like reaching a whole different level!

Romans 8:26 can apply to both praying and singing in the Spirit. I believe it is the most perfect worship to our Lord and King!

> Now in the same way the Spirit also helps our weakness; for we do not know what to pray for as we should, but the Spirit Himself intercedes for us with groanings too deep for words. (NASB)

In the same way, the Spirit helps us in our weakness, for we do not know how we should pray, but the Spirit himself intercedes for us with inexpressible groanings. (NET)

And the Holy Spirit helps us in our weakness. For example, we don't know what God wants us to pray for. But the Holy Spirit prays for us with groanings that cannot be expressed in words. (NLT)

Once you get used to singing short songs during your worship times, I would encourage you to make whole sessions out of it. When you enter into that realm with Holy Spirit, there is no telling what He will do. He may even lead you to interpret your tongues.

When you enter into that realm with Holy Spirit, there is no telling what He will do.

One day, during my alone time, I got lost worshiping in tongues. I had been singing my heart out and wasn't even paying attention to what language I was singing in. I had been practicing this form of worship for months, so it was not unusual for me to just start singing without regard to whether it was in English or other tongues. While I was singing, I noticed a melody forming. As I continued with it, I could tell that a melody was clearly present and kind of familiar.

Once I became aware of this, I turned my attention slightly toward the song itself, and I started trying to figure out the English. I was curious about where Holy Spirit was taking me. The melody became much more familiar, and I realized that I had known it in the past, but I just couldn't grasp what it was. As I continued to dig, I felt like Holy Spirit was actually playing a game with me. I think He enjoyed the game. I know I did.

Since then, there have been many times when I would realize that I was singing a song. When I have an English phrase, I'll sometimes do an online search to see if it's a song I've heard before. Sometimes it is, and sometimes it's not. One well-known song took me half an hour to figure out. It would have been easy to search online based on the line I already knew, but I refused to look it up this time. I was determined to get the song directly from Holy Spirit. He has shown me that this stubbornness is actually a strength. Basically, I just refuse to give in until He does. I'll be so bold as to say, I think He likes that about me.

Questions Answered

I encourage you to think outside the box when it comes to worshiping God. Don't limit your worship time to the four walls of a church building. You can praise Him anywhere and at any time—around the house, in the shower, in the car, while pumping gas, while walking the dog, you name it. Worship can eventually move from your alone time with Him and spill over into your daily routines. It can become a lifestyle. By worshiping Him regularly, you will make Him such a reality in your daily life that He will become your everything. Your very oxygen!

By worshiping Him regularly, you will make Him such a reality in your daily life that He will become your everything.

So to answer my questions from the start of this chapter—

What does worship look like?

It looks like a bride abandoning her whole *self* to the Bridegroom because He laid down His life for the bride. Only "the One" will do.

How do we worship now?

We can worship by constantly making ourselves aware of Jesus through the Person of Holy Spirit by turning our hearts to Him.

Does that worship look like the worship performed in the Bible?

    I believe it can!

Is there a better or more "perfect" way to worship God?

    He is perfect and calls us to perfection (the NLT calls this "spiritually mature" in Phil. 3:15). I believe perfect worship is attainable through continual heart encounters with the King.

Is He asking us to worship Him for His pleasure or for our own benefit and wellbeing?

    The One who is Glory will inevitably receive *all* glory. He doesn't "need" worship the way an earthly ruler might. I believe He receives pleasure in our worship, but His survival or security is not dependent on if we decide to worship that day.

    Worship is fully for our benefit. When His eyes of fire have so captivated your heart, you will look nowhere else for love. No other earthly possession will do. When you are so consumed with Him, you will find that He is so consumed with you. You'll refuse anything else. And you'll refuse anything less than all of Him. I would say that's pretty beneficial.

Intimacy Activation Prayer

Now, I want you to put your hand on your heart. We're just going to wipe our slates clean and start off fresh in our hearts. Say this prayer out loud.

Lord, I repent of anything that I let take up a throne in my heart. I surrender my heart fully to You; even though I might not know what that looks like, I know You are faithful to show me. I love and adore You, Lord. And I worship You now.

Practice His Presence

Although worshiping the Lord should and will become a lifestyle for you, effective worship starts with practice. Here, I would like to encourage you to use your next few alone times with the Lord to focus mainly on worship. Remember the suggested ways of worship we discussed in this chapter:

- Worship and Word
- Worship and Proclamation
- Worship and Waiting
- Worship and Fasting
- Worship in the Spirit

These are great places to start, but they are only suggestions. Worship in whatever way Holy Spirit leads. Also consider how you can incorporate the information from previous chapters on mediation, adoration, and the names of God into these worship times.

Go into your prayer closet, set a timer—or not—and lift your hands. Start out by thanking Holy Spirit for being there with you. Eloquence is not what we're after. Heartfelt worship is. Because it's hard for me to stay silent in my adoration of Him, here is an example of what I might say:

Holy Spirit, I thank You. I worship You. I thank You that I'm Yours, and You're mine. I thank you that no amount of untruth can take You away from me. I praise your name. I thank You for your role as Comforter in my life. Jesus knew how badly I would need You. He knew how vital You would be to my journey. I thank You and worship You. I cherish You, Holy Spirit. Thank You for always revealing Jesus. He is Your love and mine!

Chapter 8

Enjoying Your Time with Him

A Look at Intimacy from the Song of Solomon

*One thing I have asked of the Lord, and that I will seek: That I may dwell in the house of the Lord [in His presence] all the days of my life, to **gaze upon the beauty [the delightful loveliness and majestic grandeur]** of the Lord and to meditate in His temple. For in the day of trouble He will hide me in His shelter; **in the secret place of His tent He will hide me**; He will lift me up on a rock.*

Psalm 27:4–5 AMP

We've made it to chapter 8, and friends, this is probably the most special and unique chapter in the whole book. In fact, this entire book grew out of the revelation I'll be sharing here. Originally, I had seen this teaching as a mini-book or a pamphlet—something small and simple—that I could give away when I spoke at events. But because of how intimacy between Jesus and me has grown, I realized that there was so much more to share with you.

But it all started here.

Several years ago, I went on a missions trip to Nicaragua. It ended up being unlike any of my other trips before or since. As soon as I got there, I sensed the Lord calling me to separate myself from the group and stay in my room. I felt like I should fast and pray and just hang out with Him. I told my pastor what I was sensing, and he gave me the okay. This green light was important because I *was* in the country for missions work. The fact that my pastor was in agreement was confirmation for me.

In my room, I felt led to start reading from Song of Solomon. When I got to chapter 2, I knew that was where I needed to be. Verse-by-verse, the Lord walked me through the chapter. I sat there for days, took notes, and just talked with Him about the chapter. What I found so deep and beautiful was how the love story that unfolded between Solomon and his bride is really a picture of Jesus and His bride, the church. *Us. Me.*

I took so many notes and delved so deeply into this chapter that it is somewhat difficult to convey to a reader. But praise Holy Spirit! He is our ultimate teacher. So, I am laying this chapter out the best way I can, and I fully trust Holy Spirit to open to you what you need in your life right now. It's my hope that, through this verse-by-verse breakdown, you will see just how easy it is to enter into His presence.

I am using the New American Standard Bible (NASB) for this chapter, so I will not label it here. You are free to study from whichever version you like best. However, you may find that the subheadings in your version are different from this one or are not present at all. This is why I chose this particular version; the headings are clear: "The Groom," "The Bride," and "The Chorus."

Think of this chapter—and even the entire book of Song of Solomon—as being like a play, and the headings (in bold below) representing the individual speakers. More importantly, see "The Groom" as representing Jesus and "The Bride" as representing *you*.

Before we begin the verse-by-verse breakdown, I suggest that you read through the chapter first. You can read it in your own Bible or read the bold and italicized text throughout this chapter, skipping the explanations that follow each section... for now. When you're done, come back to this spot. And let's begin.

(The first heading of chapter 2 carries the title "The Bride's Admiration," but I have simplified it here.)

The Bride [v. 1]

> *I am the rose of Sharon,*
>
> *The lily of the valleys.*

This first verse of chapter 2 speaks of identity: Who are you? Look at what the bride is telling us by her confession. What mindset does she have as she approaches her lover? She sounds confident. We, too, must come to the Lord with confidence! Know that you are called to intimacy. He has chosen you like a person would choose a beautiful and delicate flower from a meadow.

Know that you are called to intimacy.

Romans 8:30 says, "And these whom He predestined, He also called; and these whom He called, He also justified; and these whom He justified, He also glorified" (NASB). Know that you are supposed to be in that secret, quiet, secluded place with Him. Know that you are also welcome there.

Ephesians 1:4 tells us that "He chose us in Him before the foundation of the world, that we would be holy and blameless before Him. In love." The Father has asked us to be with His Son—in love. He planned your relationship with Him before the very foundation of the world. So, we must speak it out in faith that we are sons and daughters of the Most High God. Sometimes it may seem that we are "calling those things that are not, as though they were" (see Rom. 4:17). But this is our perspective. To the Father, this is how He truly sees us. This is a reality for Him already. So, speak it and make it *your* reality.

And then come to Him with confidence and let nothing stop you: "Let us draw near with confidence to the throne of grace, so that we may receive mercy and find grace to help in time of need" (Heb. 4:16). When we approach our Beloved, we can and should do so with confidence, knowing that it is our destiny to be with Him—to behold Jesus.

The Groom [v. 2]

Like a lily among the thorns,

So is my darling among the young women.

Now it's the Groom's turn. Keeping in mind that the Groom represents Jesus, consider how tenderly He speaks of His bride—of us. Jesus is saying, "This is how I see you. You are not just a flower among flowers or a flower among the grass. You are a flower among thorns." Why is being a flower among thorns significant? It reveals that He sees you as unique and more beautiful than anything else that surrounds you. You are His diamond in the rough.

"For this is what the LORD Almighty says: 'After the Glorious One has sent me against the nations that have plundered you—for whoever touches you touches the apple of his eye" (Zech. 2:8 NIV). That's how precious you are to Him. You are the apple of

His eye. His prized possession. The psalmist understood this most special position when he pleaded, "Keep me as the apple of your eye; hide me in the shadow of your wings" (Ps. 17:8 NIV). He's calling to us: "I have called you out to bring you in. Come to Me."

The Bride [v. 3]

> *Like an apple tree among the trees of the forest,*
> *So is my beloved among the young men.*
> *In his shade, I took great delight and sat down,*
> *And his fruit was sweet to my taste.*

The bride is speaking again. The first time she spoke, she revealed that she recognized her worthiness to be in the Groom's presence. She spoke what she knew that she was to Him. In this verse, she turns the attention to her Lover, declaring who *He* is to *her*.

The bride says that her Groom is "like an apple tree." In that time period and region, apple trees were rare and precious. In fact, the Amplified Bible calls them "rare and welcome" in the forest.

The bride goes on to speak of sitting down in the shade of that tree and tastes of the fruit. She "took great delight." This sounds a lot like adoration within the secret place. Just as she recognized when she was in His presence (His shadow or shade), we should too. Experiencing His presence will look different for each of us. And the time it takes to fully enter in will also differ. But Psalm 27:14 tells us not to give up: "Wait for the LORD; be strong and let your heart take courage; yes, wait for the LORD" (NASB).

Let's talk about what happens here, in this place of resting in His presence, of adoring Him. I have learned that more happens here than can be understood or written about. But there are two things I feel it's important to highlight.

We are restored. What wrongs that have been done to you in this world are now undone: hurts, sufferings, injustices, childhood trauma, broken hearts, and so on. Situations of hurt and heartache that took years to occur are undone in moments with Abba. Because some hurts go much deeper than others, some of us may find we need to enter His presence and stay in this place of adoration more often and longer than others do. Enter often, and for however long it takes until every wall is crumbled, every stronghold is torn down, and every stone is overturned. (See 2 Cor. 10:4–5.)

We are healed. Physical and emotional healings occur when Yahweh shows up. Think of when sick people entered the presence of Jesus or when the demon-possessed encountered Him. The sickness, the demons, and even death could not escape the healing power that flowed from Him. When you enter into that same presence, expect anything and everything to happen. Have faith without limits!

I had had fibromyalgia for years, and over time, it grew severe. There were times when it was too painful to sit, stand, or even lie down. I took medication for the fibromyalgia, another medication for the pain, and another just to be able to sleep through it all.

One day, while I was spending time with the Lord, I noticed a tingling sensation in my feet, back, and other effected areas. I wasn't completely sure what was happening, but as the days and weeks went on, I continued to feel this tingling whenever I was in His presence. After a few months, I sensed a prompting from Him to stop taking my medications. I didn't know if I could do that, though. I had been on them for too long and was too dependent on them. I also wasn't certain that I was hearing from the Lord. I thought it could be my own thoughts.

After a few weeks, when the promptings didn't stop, I decided to believe that He was speaking to me. I took a step of faith and fully stopped all medications. You're probably not surprised that I have a sidenote to this. Like the topic of fasting, I am not recommending this for you. This is my personal story. If you are on medications, you should talk to your doctor, and you need to do what is right for you. The decision to make changes like this is always between the individual and God Himself. Like I said, it took weeks for me to make this decision.

It wasn't until weeks after stopping my medication, when their effects had fully worn off, that I realized what the Lord had done—what He had done through our quiet times together. He didn't just get rid of the fibromyalgia, but He took care of all the other illnesses I had been battling—mental and physical. I was completely healed! It was personal proof to me, in my own body, that He is "able to do far more abundantly beyond all that we ask or think, according to the power that works within us" (Eph. 3:20 NASB).

I am not special or unique in the fact that Jesus did this for me. This is for all of us! There is incredible power in His presence. It's important, though, not to set a timeframe on what you think He has for you. This healing in my body was progressive and took place over months. Just rest in Him and let Him do the work for you. Just keep enjoying Him.

Now, let's swing back to the last line of verse 3. The bride is enjoying the shade of the Groom and says, "His fruit was sweet to my taste." The "shade" that we enjoy is that of His presence, and it is a place for us to partake of His "cup," to drink of Him, to be filled with His living waters. His fruit is sweet and delicious. And most of all, He is satisfying. Completely fulfilling.

His fruit is sweet and delicious. And most of all, He is satisfying. Completely fulfilling.

I call verse 3 a description of His "cup" because it's kind of like the drink before a meal. When you go to someone's house for dinner, they may offer you something to drink as soon as you arrive. Or the cup could be that stage when someone is not ready for solid foods, so they start off with liquids. This "liquid" stage of His presence is a place where we can only handle His drink, the early parts of intimacy. But when the two of you are ready (and only you two will know when that is), He will lead you to the next level.

What is the next level? It is His dinner table!

The Bride [continued; v. 4]

He has brought me to his banquet hall,

And his banner over me is love.

Think of a fruit-bearing tree. The DNA of the tree is revealed by the fruit that grows from it. Since we have the Spirit of God living inside us, and since He recreated us to be like Him, His fruit is what will be revealed. Up to this point, in your intimate times with Him, you have been drinking in love, joy, peace, patience, kindness, goodness, faithfulness, gentleness, and self-control (see Gal. 5:22–23). And because you have been taking Him in, you will also be bursting with love, joy, peace, patience, kindness, goodness, faithfulness, gentleness, and self-control. You are what you partake of!

As you practice His presence, you might not notice the changes immediately, but I can bet that others will. I believe you will reach a point where any kind of striving is over. You will know that it's time to sit at His table, and you will commune with Him effortlessly.

The bride says in verse 4 that "He has brought me to his banquet hall." What does this mean for us? It means that Jesus is leading you there! It means that He wants you there—here! With Him!

"His banner over me is love." Setting a banner over someone declares him or her as the chief, highest, most exalted, or most distinguished. In Scripture, banners or flags were used during times of war. Their presence overhead gave comfort to those returning from battle and ensured protection to those within the camp.

The banner mentioned in verse 4, though, doesn't apply to just any flag. It was the type of flag that was put up over the headquarters of the king, queen, or commanding officer with a battle camp. These headquarters were the most highly guarded and protected of any area within the camp. The importance of this residence is similar to how Americans view the White House, with its flag always flying overhead.

Imagine what this means for us! The Lord of the universe is overjoyed to fly His banner over you. He comforts and protects you as you come and go from this secret place. I see this banner as His way of saying, "You are raised above all others. There is no one like you." But wait, isn't this how we see *Him*? This verse reveals how He sees you, how He feels about *you*. He says you are worthy of being at the table with Him. And He will make sure that you know it.

The New Living Translation expresses this verse beautifully: "He escorts me to the banquet hall; it's obvious how much he loves me."

The Bride [continued; v. 5]

Refresh me with raisin cakes,

Sustain me with apples,

Because I am lovesick.

Now comes the fullness of Him, the bread, the sustenance of life. His bread fills and sustains us, and it's long-lasting. This is what happens when you reach the dinner table. His drink refreshes you, and His bread strengthens you. Even though verse 5 speaks of "raisin *cakes*," it is not what we think of as cake. It is bread, real food.

Isaiah 40:31 says, "Those who hope in the LORD will renew their strength. They will soar on wings like eagles; they will run and not grow weary, they will walk and not be faint." Other versions, like the NASB, say, "Those who wait for the LORD . . ." (italics added). Waiting on the Lord is the heart of intimacy with Him. Reaching this deep level will sustain you well after you leave your time alone with the Bridegroom. Know that you can dip into His presence for a refreshing drink during your day when you miss Him. But then you can sit down at His banquet table for His bread. His table becomes your consistent craving—short visits and little snacks are not enough!

Waiting on the Lord is the heart of intimacy with Him.

When we speak of bread, it is obvious how this relates to Jesus. He declared, "I am the bread of life. Whoever comes to me will never be hungry again. Whoever believes in me will never be thirsty" (John 6:35 NLT). So I ask you: Are you coming to Him to be fed, or are you just believing *in* Him? There is a big difference.

He asked me this same question, and I could see instances in my walk with Him where I was just believing in Him. Coming to Him to be fed creates a totally different—and better—dynamic in your life.

The bride closes out this verse with, "Because I am lovesick." When I first read the way the NIV translates this phrase, "faint with love," it didn't make sense to me. I understand that Song of Solomon is a book about love. But "lovesick" and "faint with love" didn't seem to fit in this section about being strengthened with food. So I looked it up in Strong's Concordance. This phrase means to be "weak for something."

What is the bride weak for? The NLT says, "For I am weak with love." The bride is weak with love for her Groom, and the only remedy is to be fed with His bread and His drink. Is this the remedy for you too? Jesus, our lovely Groom, is the only answer to a hungry soul.

The Bride [continued; v. 6]

His left hand is under my head,

And his right hand embraces me.

This verse expresses extreme intimacy. The bride speaks of what the Groom is doing. It's not about what is happening to her, but rather, how He is handling her. How He is touching her. Why does this touching matter? Why does this even appear in the Bible? Look at the position of the Groom's hands: "Left hand . . . under my head . . . right hand embraces me." This closeness is significant. He is holding her as closely as a person can hold another. They aren't holding hands. His hand isn't even caressing her face. He has reached past her physical attributes and has wrapped himself around her, to just be with her. In this intimate embrace, they are tangled up together, lost in each other.

Get lost in Jesus! Get lost in Holy Spirit. John 16:13 calls Him the "Spirit of truth." The Good News Translation says that He reveals Jesus. Allow Holy Spirit time to paint an intimate picture of our beautiful Savior. Give Him time to reach past the outer layers of your soul and penetrate deep down.

Personally, I see verse 6 as an image of Jesus and me coming together. We are face-to-face. He is pouring His entirety into me. This can be a picture for you too. I'd like us to stop for a few minutes and practice His presence. Meditate on this verse, on this moment, and see it happening. Take your time, and then come back, and we'll move on to verse 7.

Meditate on this verse, on this moment, and see it happening.

The Groom [v. 7]

Swear to me, you daughters of Jerusalem,

By the gazelles or by the does of the field,

That you will not disturb or awaken my love

Until she pleases.

The Groom speaks again. But not to the bride. He speaks to the "daughters of Jerusalem." On first reading, it's easy to overlook this verse because it's almost anticlimactic; showing someone sleeping kind of slows down the pacing. Yet this message about not waking up the bride is said three times throughout the book (3:5; 8:4), so there must be significance to it. He says, "swear to me," or I implore you, or I beg of you. Can you feel the emotion in the Groom's words? Promise me, he says, do not "disturb or awaken my love" from her slumber. Do not pull her out of this place of rest—until she pleases."

When I read this verse in light of intimacy and spending time with Him, I see it as clearing the way for a deeper relationship with Him. At this point, we have reached a place with Him where we can be truly in His presence daily. The reason He begs us not to "disturb or awaken" is because He doesn't want things to pull us out of His rest prematurely. Those thoughts that cross your mind when you're in your prayer closet, those distractions that arise, thoughts like: What about dinner? Was that the dryer buzzing? Who's picking the kids up today? Have I fed the dog? What's happening at the office?—they all work to pull us away from that place with Him.

So when we see that this verse is repeated throughout Song of Solomon as a type of theme, it serves as a reminder that those distractions may show up, but we must and can remain focused on Jesus. How can we do that when distractions come? Something I do is ask Him, "Lord, what can I do to keep You here? Can I sing for You? Can I get on my knees and praise You? Should I lay on my face and worship You?" I'll do whatever it takes to draw further into His presence. We went over the various practices of redirection earlier in this book. But I have also found that I can sometimes just ignore the busy thoughts—I don't fight them or even cast them down. I can just embrace Jesus even more; I can sing praises to His name. And I find relief. By practicing redirection until it becomes a habit and then just learning to shift your focus to Him, I believe these trivial thoughts will stop bombarding your mind in time.

By practicing redirection until it becomes a habit and then just learning to shift your focus to Him, I believe these trivial thoughts will stop bombarding your mind in time.

The Bride [v. 8]

> *Listen! My beloved!*
>
> *Behold, he is coming,*
>
> *Leaping on the mountains,*
>
> *Jumping on the hills!*

Verse 8 is such a sweet verse. The exclamation marks make it look like the bride is shouting to anyone who will hear. But it is likely that these words actually represent her thoughts. She is thinking—complete with exclamation marks—"Listen! My beloved! He is on his way to see me!" This reveals affection with *much* anticipation. She is looking ahead to what her time with the Groom is going to be like.

We just came from verse 7, where we discussed distractions and how to deal with them while practicing His presence. Here in verse 8, Holy Spirit shows us the way back to awareness of Him; He gives us a way to refocus on Him quickly. Paul encouraged Timothy "to fan into flame the gift of God, which is in you through the laying on of my hands" (2 Tim. 1:6 NIV). Paul told Timothy to bring to remembrance the time he laid hands on him, prayed, and prophesied. In this way, he would be helping to "fan into flame" that gift. We can do the same. You can bring the thoughts of your own encounters with Jesus to the front of your mind. Think of them, and you will slip right back into the bliss that is Jesus.

Although we do not and should not live in the past, God wants us to bring some of those times forward from the past; they can inform both our present and our future. A great example of this happened to me a while ago. I was worshiping the Lord in our secret place, and Holy Spirit led me to sing the old hymn "Nothing but the Blood." The first lines say, "What can wash away my sin? Nothing but the blood of Jesus." Maybe you recognize it and are already singing it. But at that time, I had not heard the song in probably fifteen years, maybe more. Yet, instantly I knew every word. The power of the Lord was all over me, and I cried like a baby while I sang it with Him.

Later, I got online and found some YouTube videos of people singing the song. Bringing this song, which had been so prevalent in my church experience when I was a kid, back to the front of my mind was such a powerful experience. Not only did it change the trajectory of that day, but it also affected my interactions with my friends and my church going forward.

A few weeks later, I was with some friends who happened to be on the worship team at church. I told them about the song and shared with them one of the videos I had found. Apparently, it had had an effect on them as well because, the following Sunday, they put it in the song line-up! When the team started singing the song, the congregation seemed to intensify their own worship. I had never seen anything like it. When I talked to the team after service, they said the same thing—they, too, had never seen the crowd engage that strongly in worship before.

When I asked the Lord what had happened during worship that day and why moments like these were so impactful for me and for others, He showed me how bringing such things up from our past times with Him is a way to remind ourselves of the powerful times in our lives. It is like fanning into flames those experiences that we've had with Him.

What I love about verse 8 is how it reveals the speediness of this tangible awareness coming back to our remembrances. The bride says, "Leaping on the mountains, jumping on the hills!" In Hebrew, the "leaping" phrase means "to spring forward or over the roughest obstacles." And "jumping on the hills" is like sprinting over great lengths of ground. The word "jumping" means "to draw together" or "to take space or distance out of the way."

When we redirect our thoughts to Him and refocus on Him, the awareness of Him comes back fast. We slip back into Him quickly because He is always there, ever-present, waiting on us.

He eagerly desires to be with you. How do I know? Look what He said to His disciples at the Last Supper: "I have been very eager to eat this Passover meal with you before my suffering begins" (Luke 22:15 NLT). Jesus knew He was about to give Himself up, and He would be put to death. In a matter of hours! But instead of thinking of Himself and spending His last evening alone, He eagerly desired to spend time with His friends. So, how much more, on this side of the cross, does He feel this way about us—about you? He opened the door for us to have perfect, unhindered communion with Him through Holy Spirit. We can walk through that door and stay as long as we want.

The Bride [continued; v. 9]

> *My beloved is like a gazelle or a young stag.*
>
> *Behold, he is standing behind our wall,*
>
> *He is looking through the windows,*
>
> *He is peering through the lattice.*

Verse 9 continues the anticipation that was set up in verse 8. If you have ever felt "separated" from God, like there's a wall between the two of you blocking access, don't lose heart. And don't give up reaching toward Him. Verse 9 shows that there is a place to go from there. Like the bride, you have something to look forward to.

First, the Groom is standing behind a wall. Separated. But then, He is seen looking through windows. A window is still a type of wall where you cannot touch the person on the other side, but you can at least see each other. Relating this to your anticipation of Him in your secret place, know that you are close. You may still be breaking down barriers in your mind, but you are seeing Him more clearly than before.

You may still be breaking down barriers in your mind, but you are seeing Him more clearly than before.

Then the next step is the Groom "peering through the lattice." In case you are not familiar with what a piece of lattice work is, it is like a wall used in a garden, but it's not solid. It is a structure made up of thin, crisscross boards that leave numerous gaps that you can see through and reach through. The Groom peering through those gaps in the lattice work means that there is no longer a solid barrier like the window. The lattice provides the hope of a touch, a smell, a conversation.

This progression is made up of three steps—standing, looking, peering—and relates directly to our times of intimacy with Him. We may start out just standing; it may be the only thing we can do at the moment. We're standing (behind the wall) and pushing the junk aside. As the "junk" is pushed away, we are now able to see Him, to look on Him (through a window). A little more pushing, and 'we're almost there! We've pushed past the distractions and the things that weigh us down. We're peering at Jesus, looking deeply into His face, and focusing on Him. And we're not letting go.

Jeremiah 29:13 speaks of how to gaze at or to focus on Him:

And you will seek Me and find Me when you search for Me **with all your heart**. [NASB]

You will seek me and find me when you seek me **with all your heart**. [NIV]

If you look for me **wholeheartedly**, you will find me. [NLT]

This wholehearted devotion called for in the Old Testament might sound like a difficult thing to do, but I promise you, it is not. Do you know why? Because we live in the New Testament, under a new covenant. We have been made new! We have the ability already programmed into us to zero in on Him. And we can do this with confidence because we were made for Him, and He was given for us. Praise the Lord!

But wait . . . there's more! Although it makes sense that this three-step process is a way for us to get to Him, this verse is about the Groom peering in at the bride. All the bride is doing is being.

When I saw this, I asked Jesus about it. This is what He told me: "When you are going through your process, you are just breaking down barriers to get to where you can see that I am already in front of you. I always have been. I always am. And I always will be. I am always available."

After He said that, I started to see Jesus as standing in front of me, tapping his foot patiently and waiting for me. But remember, this is a progression. There is still the window. He sees us! Then—Hallelujah!—He can reach through and touch us. The unveiling of ourselves is almost complete. With this verse, He is telling us that we are so close; all the preparation time and resolve are paying off.

The Bride [quoting the Groom; v. 10]

My beloved responded and said to me,

"Arise, my darling, my beautiful one,

And come along.

The Groom is now speaking to the bride. Up to now, it feels like we've done all the work, like we've been trying to get through to Him. And maybe our work has paid off because look what happens as soon as connection is made. We hear Him speak. What a wonderful sound that is! We hear Him say, "Arise, come away with me. My fair one, the one I love, let Me carry you away."

The fact is, though, He's been speaking the whole time! What we felt was "work" was really the breaking through of all the things that have kept us from hearing that still, small voice, those sweet nothings that He's speaking only to you or to me. The hurts in our lives sometimes cause us to put up walls. And not just one wall. Some of us could put up many walls—like a labyrinth. All these barriers understandably block our view of Him. Think of the lattice wall from verse 9. These walls keep us from seeing Him clearly. All the while, He has been *always* available, *always* accessible—"a very present help in trouble" (Ps. 46:1 KJV*)*.

Now, because of the cross, all hindrances have been removed. When we understand this, we can hear Him say, "Stand up, my love, My beautiful one, and let Me show you what I have for you." The unveiling has occurred. Second Corinthians 3:16 says, "Whenever a person turns to the Lord, the veil is taken away" (NASB95).

> ***Now, because of the cross, all hindrances have been removed.***

Because the veil has been removed, all we must do is to come to Him often. To cling to Him constantly. Make your alone time a priority and make it habitual. Our Bridegroom did all the work for us by removing the veil—why would we ever allow a wall to be built in its place?

The Bride [quoting the Groom; v. 11]

"For behold, the winter is past,

The rain is over and gone.

The Groom continues with two statements about putting certain seasons behind us. While these statements seem to be about the same season, the winter and the rain, I see them as distinct seasons in a person's life. I see a person shivering and almost frozen. She hasn't felt the warmth of a person's touch in such a long time. But then she sees Jesus, and He reaches out and touches her. A tidal wave of heat washes over them both. It's that first love all over again.

As for the rain. We have all experienced those times of sitting by the window, watching the rain run down the glass, and just feeling "stuck." We're locked inside. But then the sun peeks through the cloud. Jesus is that sunshine. He's outside, waiting. And now He declares that the rain is past.

The winter is over! The rain is gone! You are through those seasons. You are past the feeling of being cold. You are past the gloom and being stuck inside. You can now find joy in His presence. We are not meant to live without regularly feeding on the Bread of Life. And we cannot survive without heart encounters with the Lord. Sometimes we go through seasons without "feeling" His presence. But we must still come to Jesus by faith and know that He is (see Heb. 11:6).

Holy Spirit is saying, "The rain is over and gone. You no longer need to feel like you are stuck on the inside while I am on the outside. I am here now."

The Bride [quoting the Groom; v. 12]

"The blossoms have already appeared in the land;

The time has arrived for pruning the vines,

And the voice of the turtledove has been heard in our land.

Where verse 11 talked about the seasons that have passed, verse 12 speaks of the new season that is here. The Groom declares that the flowers are blossoming and the birds are singing! He is essentially telling the bride that they are now face-to-face; he has broken through; they are connected!

Think of when you were on a long road trip, and all you wanted was just to reach your destination. You may have fueled up a dozen times, eaten in places that were questionable, and slept in hotels that didn't feel like home. You just wanted to be "there." And then, finally, you arrived. You stepped out of the car and stretched, and it was like you could hear angels singing. The air felt—and even tasted—fresh.

The angels singing is the picture I got when I read, "the voice of the turtledove has been heard." The sound is symbolic of the celebration that happens because we have finally reached our destination in this life—His Presence. Right here on earth. This verse shows that this is a time to rejoice and sing praises.

The Bride [quoting the Groom; v. 13]

"The fig tree has ripened its fruit,

And the vines in blossom have given forth their fragrance.

Arise, my darling, my beautiful one,

And come along!"

Look at what has happened as a result of the bride being in the presence of the Groom. The fig tree has fruit, and the vines have blossomed. What are the results of *your* being in the presence of God? Do you feel refreshed and renewed in the Father's presence? Do you feel fulfilled?

Think of the fig tree in Matthew 21 and Mark 11. Jesus walked up to it expecting fruit. It had leaves, which indicated that it should have had fruit. But there wasn't any. A fruit tree with no fruit is outside the will of God. It was out of line with how God had created it, so Jesus cursed it. Now notice that the tree in Song of Solomon 2 has budded and ripened its fruit *in one verse*. Think about that. What we strive to accomplish in the flesh, what may take years for us to do, the Lord can do in only moments of being alone with Him. He will make you grow and bud and produce matured fruit in a shorter time than you can imagine!

He will make you grow and bud and produce matured fruit in a shorter time than you can imagine!

Let's look at John 15:5–7 in the NASB95:

I am the vine, you are the branches; **he who abides in Me** and I in him, he bears much fruit, for **apart from Me you can do nothing**. If anyone does not abide in Me, he is thrown away as a branch and **dries up**; and they gather them, and cast them into the fire and they are burned. If you abide in Me, and My words abide in you, ask whatever you wish, and it will be done for you.

So, He is the vine, and I am a branch. If I remain in Him, *then* I will bear much fruit. I can only bear fruit in Him because apart from Him, I can do nothing. Some would argue that, on account of being saved, they are already abiding. While this is true, it's worth noting the two-fold process laid out in this verse: Him in me and I in Him. Jesus is always in us. He promised to never leave us, never forsake us. But Jesus purposely gave us a role. We must abide in Him! I believe this means there is a diligence on my part to stay close to Him. There is something that *I* can or cannot do, meaning that I am the variable. If we are born again, He is in us, but we also must remain.

The passage in John goes on to say that a branch that does not remain in Him "dries up." Other versions say "withers." A dried-up, withered branch is not a healthy one. Again, Jesus presents the idea that we, as the variables, can make choices that will lead to our withering and drying up. When we don't make time for the source of life—Jesus the Vine—we are choosing to wither away.

Since most of us are not vineyard keepers, we may view this vine-and-branches analogy as something abstract. So, let's look at something more concrete. Let's talk about your phone. We have all been there. It's the end of a day, you come home and set your phone down by your keys—or you hang onto your phone and spend the evening mindlessly scrolling—and then you go to bed. The next morning, you grab your phone and head out the door when you suddenly remember that you didn't plug it in. There's the wall outlet. There's the charger. And there's your phone. But you forgot to connect them. Now, you have a full day ahead of you where you're going to be dealing with a weak or, worse, a dead battery.

The passage in John is not talking about salvation; it is talking about bearing fruit, which is directed toward Christians. So, we can be Christians who produce fruit or Christians who don't. We can remain, or we can choose to cut ourselves off from the Source, the One who gives us life and strength.

Now notice another result of the mutual abiding (you in Him and He in you): "Ask whatever you wish, and it will be done for you." If I remain in His presence, I am promised that what I ask *will* be done. Why is this so simple for Him to do in this moment? Because I am with Him, right there, in His presence. The two of us have connected, and He is making Himself more real to me than reality itself. More real than the floor beneath my knees or the air I breathe. I find it easy to see a prayer request answered when I am abiding to this degree.

Remember, we are still studying the depiction of the Lord's love for us as seen through chapter 2 of Song of Solomon. So discussing abiding in Him and bearing fruit might seem like a sidenote. But look at what Jesus said a few verses down. He explains *why* He brought up the issue. "These things I have spoken to you so that My joy may be in you, and that your joy may be made full" (John 15:11 KJV).

He urges you to abide with Him, to "Arise . . . and come along" with Him for *your* benefit. So *you* may have joy to the fullest degree. So, rather than seeing abiding as a "doing," see it as a "being" or a getting to be. We get to be with Him. We have full access to Him and can spend intimate times in His presence. And when we just "be" with Him, how can we *not* be full of joy?

Let's wrap up verse 13. The Groom says, "Arise." And He calls us His "darling" and "beautiful one." Once again, He has turned the tables on us. Beautiful One is how *I see Him!*

"Arise, my darling . . . and come along!" You can't miss the excitement in those words!

Come away with me, Jesus! My beautiful Jesus! Take me deeper, deeper in You. Take me to your secret places!

The Groom [v. 14]

> *My dove, in the clefts of the rock,*
>
> *In the hiding place of the mountain pathway,*
>
> *Let me see how you look,*
>
> *Let me hear your voice;*
>
> *For your voice is pleasant,*
>
> *And you look delightful.*

Over the last few verses, the bride has been quoting the Groom. Now we hear directly from him. And look at the focus of his words. It's the bride. It's us!

As the Groom calls out to the bride who is hidden away, we can hear Jesus calling to us: "Oh, my love [that's you], you who are hiding away [seeking Him], you who are setting yourself apart in the secret place, in the quiet place, in the secluded place, let Me see your face; let Me hear your voice."

He is asking you to show Him your heart and to reveal your innermost self to Him. When we seek the face of Jesus, we are seeking His heart. In this place, He is asking the same of you. He knows your heart, but He desires such a relationship that He asks you to show it to Him. He says, "I know everything about you, but please share yourself with Me nevertheless." I can hear the desire, the longing, the pleading in His voice.

As the Groom calls for the bride to come out of hiding and show herself, hear Jesus asking you to do the same. Unveil yourself. Let Him see you. Let Him hear your voice. Your voice is beautiful to Him, and your appearance brings Him great delight!

The Chorus [v. 15]

> *Catch the foxes for us,*
>
> *The little foxes that are ruining the vineyards,*
>
> *While our vineyards are in blossom.*

Bible translations differ on who is speaking in verse 15. "The Chorus" could be a group of people, or it could simply be the part of a song that repeats after each verse. Some versions attribute this to a group watching from the outside, while others say the Groom is still speaking. Regardless of who is speaking, we can sense the urgency in this verse.

Jesus is saying that our love is blossoming. Our time is developing. We have found each other. Don't allow yourself to be stolen away from Me so quickly. Catch the foxes that ruin what is growing in such health.

We can think of these "little foxes" as something to be captured, as our biggest enemy within our secret place. They are the thoughts that aim to derail us and to steal from us. Don't think that you have no control over those foxes, though. The first word of this verse is "Catch." It's a command, something that you can do. Although you will find it easier over time to redirect yourself back to Jesus, you have to start somewhere. When a thought comes, just say no. 'If the thought (or another) comes back, again, say "No, I'm here to be with Jesus right now."

So, why "the chorus"? If we see the chorus as a repetitive refrain, then it would stand to reason that it is something that must be repeated in our own lives. Distractions, the "foxes," will be determined to interrupt our time with Him. Over and over. But we must mindful of the foxes, and we must catch them. And with His help, we can!

The Bride [v. 16]

My beloved is mine, and I am his;

He pastures his flock among the lilies.

Jesus is mine, and I am His. What a beautiful place to be! It's a place beyond the reality of this world. It is living in His presence. This is where He feeds you, in the "clefts of the rock, in the secret places of the stairs" (v. 14 KJV). Everything is coming together; everything is coming to fruition. "The LORD is my shepherd, I lack nothing. He makes me lie down in green pastures, he leads me beside quiet waters, he refreshes my soul. He guides me along the right paths for his name's sake" (Psalm 23:1–3 NIV). There is comfort in knowing everything is complete in Jesus.

Jesus is mine, and I am His. What a beautiful place to be!

Verse 16 speaks of the Groom spending time "among the lilies." Second Chronicles 16:9 says, "The eyes of the Lord run to and fro throughout the whole earth to show Himself strong in behalf of those whose hearts are blameless toward Him" (AMPC). I believe that He is looking for pure, unadulterated lovers who will radically follow Him. In myself, I am nothing. Without His blood, we are nothing. But in Him, we have a purity, a holiness. The lilies that the Lord is moving among are white; they are pure. Jesus has made you pure, spotless, and white as snow. He loves to spend time with you. Accept it. Agree with Him. And then fully enjoy your relationship with Him.

It's no surprise that this chapter of Song of Solomon ends with the Groom (Jesus) searching for a pure bride. Revelation 19 reveals that the bride has made herself ready for marriage, and verse 8 says that "to her was granted that she should be arrayed in fine linen, clean and white: for the fine linen is the righteousness of saints" (KJV). The New Living Translation says, "She has been given the finest of pure white linen to wear." The fine linen represents the righteousness that we have been clothed with. The Lord's righteousness. Walking in the understanding that you are righteous and pure through the sacrifice of the most precious Groom, Jesus will change your future.

The Bride [continued; v. 17]

> *Until the cool of the day, when the shadows flee,*
>
> *Turn, my beloved, and be like a gazelle*
>
> *Or a young stag on the mountains of Bether.*

Christ will come over every separating mountain to take us home to Himself. We can tell Him, "I know You will come for me. I know that You will meet me, and I will meet You. You will cross any river, overcome any obstacle for me. Your reckless love is my love.

Remember that the title of chapter 2 is "The Bride's Admiration." The Bridegroom, Jesus, is looking for a bride in naked admiration for Him. Unhindered, raw, sold-out affection for the One who is Love.

Intimacy Activation Prayer

Pray your own words or use what I have here. But let's pray and put off the old mindset and put on a new—perhaps very different—mindset.

Jesus, there is a love story for the two of us to walk out. I pray you show me, speak to me, teach me, and guide me. Form me into the lover You so desire me to be. Oh, returning Bridegroom! How I wait for Your day, Your special day of glory! Until that day, I simply ask that You show me what a true lover looks like and who I can become to You. Teach me how to dance with You, You who is altogether lovely.

Practice His Presence

Consider the depth of imagery found in Song of Solomon. In chapter 2, the Bridegroom is called or described as the Groom, my beloved, a gazelle, a young stag, an apple tree; he is seen leaping on mountains, jumping on hills, and pasturing his flock among lilies.

You may want to bring Song of Solomon into your secret place today, or go without it and just allow Holy Spirit to lead your time. Also, consider leaving your timer untouched and just see what Holy Spirit wants to do.

Tell the Bridegroom who He is to you. Speak the names or descriptions out loud. Choose words in your own language or in your prayer language that express the revelation that you have of Jesus. As you speak His names, His Person is made more real to you, and His presence becomes more tangible. Your adoration of Him magnifies Him in your heart and increases the revelation of who He is. As deeper revelation and understanding come to you, speak that out loud. It's a beautiful cycle.

I urge you to not leave this place of adoration until you absolutely have to. He will make Himself more real to you here than ever.

Chapter 9

Experience His Power in Personal Ways

Multiple Ways to Practice His Presence

I ask only one thing from the Lord. This is what I want: Let me live in the Lord's house all my life. Let me see the Lord's beauty. Let me look around in his Temple. During danger he will keep me safe in his shelter. He will hide me in his Holy Tent. Or he will keep me safe on a high mountain.

Psalms 27:4–5 ICB

Practice His Presence

Before we begin this chapter, I want you to pause and think about what you have read up to now. How have you changed? Do you see your relationship with Jesus differently?

Instead of waiting until the end of the chapter for our "practice," I want to start out with it. And I want you to worship Him without words. That's the phrase that stands out to me—worship Him without words. Find a place where you can experience quiet for a few minutes, whether that's your prayer closet or your empty living room. Set a timer, or don't. This time is just yours and

His. You're going to do this in silence—no music, no spoken words. This is all from the heart.

Turn your heart to Jesus. Lift your hands. And experience Him.

Thank You, Jesus.

Be appreciative of who He is. Be grateful that He is there with you right now.

I love You, Jesus.

Don't be afraid to sit in front of Him quietly. Linger with Him.

Thank You, Jesus . . .

Something that cannot be taught is how to turn your heart to Him. It's something you have to do for yourself. You open your own heart to Him. For myself, I have found that sitting in silence has helped me in this area. Sitting in silence with Holy Spirit can change your life. Don't ever be afraid of it.

The Practicals and the Experiences

I am extremely excited about what I'm going to be sharing with you here! I promised the Lord that, when I wrote this book, I would be more transparent than I've ever been regarding the "secret place." I promised Him that I would not only tell you what I have found in that place, but I would model it for you as well.

This wasn't an easy promise to make, though. Of course, everybody has that private part of them that they don't want to share. I do too. But this isn't about privacy. My concern is about you. I don't want to encourage you or anyone to chase experiences.

Seek Him. Seek Jesus. Never the experience. Don't ever stray from that. Seek Him!

This chapter is organized differently from the others. As you work your way through it, I want you to be free to lay the book down at any point and go "practice." Don't wait for the end of the chapter to Practice His Presence. I urge you to read the chapter with an attitude of worship and adoration, with your heart turned toward Him. Listen for His leading. If He says, "Let's sit together," then do it. Right then. Jesus is always there when *you* need Him. Be willing to extend the same to Him.

Another thing that makes this organization different involves the practical tips and the experiences themselves. You can almost view this chapter as part "how-to" and part "memoir." In my practices—sitting quietly, meditation, worship, fasting, and so on—I have experimented with various things: how long to set the timer, to ditch the timer completely, fast for hours or only certain meals or certain foods, singing in my known language or singing in my prayer language, memorizing Scripture, meditating on phrases. The list could go on. The point is that over time, I began to experience Him in supernatural ways. When this happened, I would look back over my journal to see what I was doing before this encounter occurred. This is what I have compiled to share with you.

Although I don't want to bog you down with unnecessary details, I feel those seemingly little details—what I was doing, where I was, how long I was there—have made the difference for me. The details I'm sharing are not prescribed recipes. Please don't think that if you do the exact same things, you will have the exact same results. But I offer these details for you to grab some ideas for yourself and to tell the Lord, "I'm taking this for *me*. Show me what this looks like for *me*."

This chapter also lends itself well to journaling. Whether in the accompanying prayer journal or in your own notebook, write down the ideas that come to you under each "Practical." Ideas can slip away as quickly as they come, so I urge you to capture them right away.

Practical 1: Find what works for you.

As you read along, I want you to practice with me. But then, it will be *your* responsibility to find out how He wants you to get alone with Him. It's your job to decide if being on your knees in front of Him is best for you or if you'd rather stand. Do you like sitting in your recliner or stretching out on your couch? Do these positions cause you to fall asleep every time? This is where your active participation comes in. Consider reviewing chapter 2; it contains numerous tips about this very thing.

Practical 2: Create an itinerary. Leave something blank.

There is nothing wrong or unspiritual about planning your prayer time. Creating a plan or "itinerary" can give you a way to focus that time. It can keep you from becoming distracted. Of course, following the leading of Holy Spirit is always key to our times with Him, which is why I recommend leaving a portion of your plan blank—a place that only He can fill.

The night prior to one of my most memorable encounters with the Lord, He and I came up with an itinerary of what the following day would look like. He had previously spoken to me about creating this type of schedule for our alone time so I would have a clearer picture of how to focus the time. As I wrote the list, I got the impression that there were three things. I wrote the first two, but the third thing was elusive. I wrote "3," left the line blank, and went to bed.

Experience—The Most Memorable Encounter

The next day was "our day." I had taken the day off from work, and after dropping my girls off at school, I had no other obligations. I was beside myself with excitement and expectation. I was fully expectant to follow our itinerary. And I was fully expectant that the Lord would show up. I see this as that childlike faith that Jesus talks about. I have learned that this type of faith is extremely important—it's just a *knowing* when you enter that secret place. It's an expectancy.

The first two items on the itinerary were very specific. The first thing I would do would be to play an hour-long worship DVD. I would worship with my hands up and possibly be on my knees, though I was open to moving around. The second thing on my list was praying in the Spirit. The plan was that after the one hour of worship, I would pray in my prayer language for at least an hour. These are the items I wrote down.

So, I played the DVD and worshiped for a total of one hour and twenty minutes. Then I shifted to my prayer language and prayed for about forty-five minutes—that I know of. Somewhere between forty-five minutes and an hour is when He came into the room!

I was praying when I felt something in the room shift. My eyes were closed, so I couldn't see anything, but I could feel it—

something had changed. I thought the Lord had actually walked through several walls and through my front door. His presence was that real. To be honest, even though I was expectant, I was a little freaked out because I had never felt anything like this before. I stayed calm and continued to pray quietly.

A few minutes later, I sensed an increase in the intensity of the "presence." I knew that whoever had come into the room had just come closer. Up to that point, I hadn't opened my eyes. I guess I was afraid I would lose the feeling or something. But as He got closer, I decided to peek. I saw Him, and yet, I didn't see Him. I saw nothing with my physical eyes. But the spiritual realm became more real to me than anything I had ever experienced. I knew this was a special moment, and I knew in that instant how truly special He is!

I wasn't peeking anymore. For the rest of the time, I kept my physical eyes closed. It was as if I didn't need them. The Lord walked from my right side and stood in front of me. It felt like He was about three feet away. Even though that's a physical measurement, it just felt right. I could see things I'd never seen before; I could feel things I had never felt before. And then we began to talk.

We had a real and lengthy conversation. I asked Him countless questions, and He answered them. He asked me questions, too, so I answered them. That part is almost funny to say, because why would God need to ask me things? He knows everything. I have learned so much on this journey of intimacy, but one of the biggest things I've learned is that intimacy takes two. He truly is a Bridegroom. And He wants to know everything about me.

I have learned so much on this journey of intimacy, but one of the biggest things I've learned is that intimacy takes two.

Just like I didn't see Him with my physical eyes, I didn't hear Him speak with my physical ears. In fact, His words were visual! I mean, who has ever *seen* spoken words? I did that day. His words kind of flew or floated around the room. I could sense that the words had purpose and drive. They were full of destiny. They weren't like words on a chalkboard—one-dimensional and flat. I saw these words spelled out in block letters, with height, length, and width . . . and depth.

I mentioned something from this conversation back in chapter 4. But that day, I asked Him, "Why is it so hard to get here? Why does it seem like I have to wait forever to get to You, to reach you like in this moment?" Here is what I recorded in my journal:

March 2: What He said came so alive to me that I collapsed and shook all over. It was so simple. He said, "I've been waiting for you, for *this*, for 2,000 years." And in that moment, I could see, feel, and experience the longing He has for us. The desire to see us put everything else aside and say, "This time is Yours and no one else's."

When He spoke those words, they went through me with such intense love... anticipation... so many indescribable feelings. But with those words also came some visuals—this time, they weren't visuals of the words themselves. They were of my cells. I had asked the Lord why I was shaking. He showed me my cells literally reaching out with everything they had to be one with Him. To touch Him. Every one of them was crying out to Him.

Practical 3: Set an expectation level each night.

Whether you have or have not had an intense encounter like the one I described, expect something and don't stop expecting. Every night when you go to bed, write an itinerary, or at the very least, tell the Lord, "When I step into my quiet place, Lord, I know you're going to be there. Throughout my day tomorrow, You're going to be there."

After such a memorable encounter with the Lord, things changed in me. For a while, I continued writing and following an itinerary. Every day, I set aside time to be with Him. Each day, I dropped my daughters off at school; I practically rushed home so He and I could pick up where we left off. There was such an expectancy in me now. I have told people that I became addicted to Him. I still am.

Practical 4: "Fast" *time* and ditch the itinerary.

I believe that "fasting" means to give up food for a time. In my opinion, giving up anything else is more of a "discipline" than a fast. However, for the sake of an easy description, I call this method "fasting time"—meaning, I give up some of my time. Usually, it's time that I would have spent sleeping or doing some other routine. For you, it may be time spent with the television, social media, or a hobby. It's that "me time" that I'm talking about.

Don't feel like you must keep to your new schedule forever. If it was forever, it wouldn't be a fast. It would just be your normal schedule. Fast your decided-upon time for a few days, weeks, or whatever you feel called to. Then when that time is done, simply go back to your normal schedule just like you would do if you had been fasting food.

Experience—Office Encounter Teaser

During a period when I was fasting time, I started getting up at four in the morning. The rest of the family got up at six, so this gave me two hours every morning to spend with the Lord in the word. After a while of these two-hour-a-day Bible-reading sessions, I sensed the Lord say, "When are you going to give *Me*, the Living Word, some time?" Immediately I thought, *I am*; I wouldn't be giving up two hours of sleep every day for no reason. I had heard that to spend time in the Bible is to spend time with Him. And, in a way, this is true. But at that point, I didn't understand His question. I was actually kind of confused about it. So instead of asking Him to explain, I just went on doing what I was doing.

One morning, before I got started, I asked the Lord, "What's on Your heart today? What would You have me do?" His answer was crystal clear: "One hour of praying in tongues, then one hour in the word." That's when I realized what He had been trying to tell me. Spending time in the word is good. But the word should always lead us to the Person of Christ. If we are reading our Bibles just for the sake of reading our Bibles, then we are missing the true intimacy we could be enjoying with Him.

It took some practice and a lot of cough drops to get up to one hour of praying. After all, it was early in the morning, I was giving up sleep, and I was not used to talking that much, even during the day. (I'm going to sneak another tip in here. If one hour sounds impossible for you, try this: Set a timer and pray for fifteen minutes. Then reset that timer and pray for another fifteen minutes. Do that a total of four times. Repeat that process for a few days, and you should start to see how quickly one hour goes by.)

So, I started with one hour of praying in the Spirit and then one hour in the word. Exactly thirty days into this schedule . . .

Well, the word *teaser* in the heading should tell you that I'm saving this full experience for a little later in the chapter.

Practical 5: Use a devotional or Bible promises book.

Find a daily devotional book written by a preacher or ministry you trust. Or get a Bible promises or topical Scripture book. Read something from it daily. This doesn't take the place of your alone time with God or your regular Bible reading, but a good devotional and certainly a promises book will have bite-sized Scripture passages that you can ponder and meditate on. It's also one way to keep things fresh. It reminds me of how God provided manna for the Israelites in the wilderness. He gave them fresh manna every day. Like them, we need fresh manna daily instead of living off the old.

Experience—Learning from My Daily Devotional

I have a favorite devotional. It uses a mixture of quoted and paraphrased Scripture. But the daily devotions are short and to the point. I can get through one quickly, or if I want to take more time, I pour over the quoted Scripture, look up the references, and just enjoy the word. Often, when I read it, I get a timely revelation—the very thing I needed for that day.

One devotional I read was all about waiting and the difficulties that sometimes go along with that waiting. As you and I both have probably grown to believe, waiting, sitting, not doing anything seems counterproductive; it's the opposite of what the world does. If something needs to be done, why wait around? Shouldn't I just go and do it? Get 'er done! But when I think of what I've seen in the Bible, I can't think of one person who just went out and did something great without first seeking God. To do and to be great in Him requires waiting on Him in that quiet, secret place."

Practical 6: Play a variety of music.

Songs, soaking music, and hymns. This is similar to "Practical 1: Find what works for you." The music you play may change from day to day or from week to week. Sometimes, I listen to music from my favorite worship bands and worship along. Other times I find "soaking music" online and play it in a continual loop. I have also found hymns from past decades and centuries to be exactly what I need to hear at various times.

Songs. Sing the songs you've learned in church. Pick one or two songs with simple lyrics, something easy to memorize. My favorite to sing without having to dig deeply to remember is called "I Love Your Presence." The chorus literally contains those four words from the title and the name *Jesus,* and that's it. The melody is easy to remember, and the repetition of the words make it a great one to just let go of self and worship Him. If you don't know this one, then think of one you do know, and take a moment right now. Pause for a few minutes, close your eyes, turn your heart to Him, and sing.

Soaking music. There are so many kinds of soaking music you can find online. I search "soaking worship music" and can find any number of videos labeled and organized by length. These instrumental tracks are a collection of songs that you may even recognize. This gives you background music that you can sing along with or just allow to "soak" the room. In my times with the Lord, I choose a music video based on the length of time I plan to worship or pray or read the word, etc. When the music reaches its end, if I'm not done, I just swipe or click it back to the beginning and replay it.

Hymns. I have found old hymns to be powerful in my worship times. Although I find many of the hymns online, I also like to sing straight from a hymnal. I bought one for myself, and I love looking through it and singing those anointed songs. I find the hymns simple to sing and memorize, like modern worship choruses, which make it easier for me to fully focus on Jesus. To learn the value of hymns for yourself, search online for the "top 25 hymns of all time" or something similar. You may be surprised when you see that some of them were written as early as the 1500s! You may even notice that they sound a little familiar. Many modern worship groups will adapt an old hymn to a newer sound. You may have even sung it in church last Sunday!

Practical 7: Pray as Holy Spirit leads.

It is no secret that I believe in the baptism of Holy Spirit with the evidence of speaking in tongues. I would be lost without this form of prayer. Praying in my prayer language, as Holy Spirit leads, allows me to let go of mental distractions and just focus on Him. Because soaking music has no words, I can sing along to the melody in my prayer language and just get lost in Him. I do the same thing with hymns. I use the melody but pray in other tongues. Again, this is as the Spirit leads.

I also pray this way in my car. Allowing Holy Spirit to lead gives me the opportunity to focus on my driving while also focusing on Him. I don't have to think about the words I'm going to say; I'm not reading from a long prayer list, I just pray in the language He has given me, and I flow with Him.

I don't have to think about the words I'm going to say; I'm not reading from a long prayer list, I just pray in the language He has given me, and I flow with Him.

As you pray and as you worship, also consider varying the speed at which you pray. Slow things way down, even to the point that it feels uncomfortable. When you sing, slow it down. This forces pauses in your speaking or singing, allowing Him to slip in and surprise you.

Practical 8: Eat before you go in or eat with the Lord.

Have you ever heard the statement that someone is so heavenly minded that he's no earthly good? In this study of intimacy, I have talked about turning our hearts toward Jesus, ignoring distractions, meditating on Scripture, and so much more that it can seem like we're required to deny the physical—both our physical needs and the physical realm. But let's face it. Sometimes our legs cramp up when we kneel for a long time. Sometimes we fight (and lose the battle to) sleep. And sometimes we just get hungry.

My advice to you is, before you go into your secret place with the Lord, assess your plans for that time with Him. If you use a timer, you already have an idea of how long you plan to spend there. You 'know your internal schedule and how you feel at that time of day. If you think that one of these physical needs may be sending you signals during your time with Him, then take care of it beforehand. And if your time in your prayer closet lasts longer than you had planned, talk to God about it. He made you. He knows your every need.

Experience—Eating with the Lord

There have been many times I got hungry during my alone time with Him. Although I've learned to eat before I go in, sometimes it still happens, especially when the time goes longer than I expected. One of those times, I had found myself about four hours into alone time with the Lord, and I was hungry. *Really* hungry. I didn't want my time with the Lord to stop, but the hunger wasn't going away. So I talked to Him about it. It's not unusual that I would talk to Him about my lunch. I try to talk to Him about everything. But this time alone with Him was so special, I didn't want a simple thing like a sandwich to interrupt even a moment of it.

I went in into the kitchen to make lunch, and He stayed with me. I felt Him all over me, so tangibly. I moved through preparing lunch slowly—I didn't know what else to do. It was such a holy moment. I sensed His pleasure with me, and I truly felt like we had lunch together. Afterwards, we went right back to the closet together and continued our time.

I can honestly say it's unique what you'll go through with Him as you grow in intimacy with Him. What I have experienced is so humbling and amazing! He's such a lovely person to be with.

Practical 9: Accumulate the "practicals."

I have shared several practical tips that I have learned over time. As I said before, much of these came about through experimentation and just learning how to flow with Holy Spirit. I talked about creating an itinerary, daily expecting to meet with Him, "fasting" time, using a devotional and a variety of music, and more. In your time working through this book, I pray you have experienced more of Him. But I also want to assure you that if you haven't sensed a noticeable difference yet, don't give up! He is faithful. Remember what I said back in chapter 4: He wants to be with you more than you want to be with Him. Personal encounters will eventually happen.

For me, one of the most intense encounters I have had with Him came about after a month of fasting time. Now notice that it was exactly thirty days after I started giving up sleep to spend more time with Him, but I had already been spending time with Him daily. I had already been meditating on Scripture, worshiping Him, and falling deeper in love with Him. So, when I started fasting those two hours of sleep every day, I was adding to what I had already been doing. It was a sort of accumulation, a lifestyle of intimacy, that pushed things over.

But why a whole month? I thought I was waiting on Him—kind of like waiting for Him to give *me* His time. But He showed me that I needed to give Him *my* time so He could break things off of me. I have now realized that when I do these things every day and allow them to accumulate, it enables me to break through the feeling of always trying to get to Him. Instead, I now see Jesus pursuing me, Him nudging me, and Him coming to me. It's the complete opposite of what I used to feel. I believe it will happen for you, too! It may take some time, but I believe it will happen. Again, don't give up!

I now see Jesus pursuing me, Him nudging me, and Him coming to me. It's the complete opposite of what I used to feel.

Experience—Office Visit

I'll never forget that day. Thirty days into my "fast" of time, I was in my office at home. I had been playing soaking worship music for an hour and praying. When the music ended, I asked Him, "Do you want me to continue or go to the next thing on my itinerary?" He didn't answer with words. He answered with . . .

Him. The best way I can describe it is He came into the room like a wind.

I was sitting on the couch in my office with my eyes closed when He walked into the room. I replayed the song for another hour. I just sat there on my couch with Him the entire time. I never saw Him visibly, but I knew He was there. His fragrance was so sweet! And we sat there and ministered to each other.

Experience—Time Jump

Sometime later, after another stretch of fasting my time and other things, I had another encounter that was even more amazing. It was such a miraculous encounter that I find it hard to even describe.

This time, I was in my office at work, and I was spending time with the Lord. I worked for my church and Bible school, so praying and worshiping God in my office was not only accepted but was expected. It was on-the-clock time for me to get full and stay full. Even though I had other work to do, during my prayer time, I could lay work aside and become fully captivated by Him.

I remember the specific time He showed up because, when I started an hour-long soaking song on my computer, I had glanced at the clock. I wanted to know when I needed to get back to work, and

I also had to pick my girls up from school that day. I was going to make the most of my hour with Him because I could sense Him, then and there, wanting to be with me. I told Him, "I'm not missing this! You are here. I'm going to commune with You and worship You." So I did.

And then He showed up. The best way I can describe it is He came into the room like *fire*! I felt Him, and I saw Him . . . like He was wrapped in fire. I shut and locked the door, got on my knees, and worshiped.

After the hour-long song ended, I felt it was time to get back into . . . reality? I started moving around and, in the process, I looked at the clock. No time had passed! The one-hour song had played through, and I worshiped during that time, yet no time had passed. Whether He had made time stand still or had moved me backwards into time—I don't know what happened. He had come into the room, changed my life, yet I didn't miss a beat!

What had led up to this experience wasn't any one thing. In fact, that day, I was just working, like I did every day. But over the weeks prior, I was fasting food off and on. I was abstaining from all TV and social media. And, like I said, I was also fasting time, so I was getting only a few hours of sleep each night. I just had a cry in my heart for "more" of Jesus; it was a desire that I just couldn't tuck away!

Experience—Another Time Jump

I never went after that kind of experience then or since. Like I have urged you, I don't go after experiences. Even though I want more of Him, and I cry out for more of Him, I am open to Him revealing Himself in any way He wants. To be honest, I love to be surprised.

But a similar experience with time occurred about two and a half years later. Throughout my workday, I had been worshiping, praying, and just having a lot of fun with the Lord. The day hadn't been much different from any other. At the end of the day, I left work at my usual time. I distinctly remember leaving the building at a specific time. I drove home, pulled into the driveway, and looked at my watch. It read an hour and fifteen minutes earlier. I thought something was wrong with it. So I looked at my dashboard clock. The clock and my watch matched. But they didn't match up to when I left work.

I walked into my house and straight to my kitchen. The clock on my stove also read the earlier time. I knew what time I should have arrived home based on when I left work and the length of my drive. But time seemed to have gone backwards. It was literally an hour and fifteen minutes earlier than it should have been.

Living and working in a big city usually means a lot of time on the road. While some people complain about long commutes, I see my time in the car differently. In fact, my car had become a very special place for the Lord and me. Like I do with my prayer closet times, I like to set an expectation with Him when I drive. This particular day, as I got in my car to begin my drive home, I fully expected Him to show up. I just knew He was going to be there.

I started driving, and sure enough, Holy Spirit showed up. We worshiped *together* and lifted up Jesus. Holy Spirit has taught me so much, but one thing I sensed from this special experience was how He took (and continues to take) me deeper and deeper into the world of worshiping Jesus. I'm finding that there is so much depth still to be reached in our times of worship. One of those things is learning to worship *alongside* Holy Spirit as we lift up the One whom He adores—Jesus.

This commuter time jump was similar to the one that happened in my office. It was like the Lord appreciated the time I gave to Him, so He gave that time back to me. Our always-giving Lord is still giving and giving . . .

Examples from Scripture

I don't know how to explain these things. All I can say is that as we abide in Him, things are going to happen. You cannot enter His presence and not be changed. Go after Him, not things, not experiences. He is the One we go after. He's the One we love and adore.

However, manipulating time is not beyond God. He goes beyond time and distance. If He desires to change our environment for His purposes, He can do it. What He did for me was on a very small scale (though it was huge to me!). But He stopped the sun itself for Joshua and the armies of Israel.

Joshua 10:12–13 says,

> Then spake Joshua to the Lord in the day when the Lord delivered up the Amorites before the children of Israel, and he said in the sight of Israel, Sun, stand thou still upon Gibeon; and thou, Moon, in the valley of Ajalon. **And the sun stood still, and the moon stayed**, until the people had avenged themselves upon their enemies. Is not this written in the book of Jasher? So **the sun stood still in the midst of heaven, and hasted not to go down about a whole day**.

Joshua prayed and then commanded the sun to stand still. This was an astronomical event that gave Joshua and his army several more hours to win the battle. But how does that explain my "minor" subtraction of time?

God manipulating time for personal reasons is answered in the story of King Hezekiah when Isaiah told him that he was going to die. Hezekiah prayed, and God heard Him. The Lord told Isaiah to tell the king that He was giving him several more years. And if the prophet's message was not enough, God gave Hezekiah proof that the words were true.

> And this shall be a sign unto thee from the LORD, that the LORD will do this thing that he hath spoken; Behold, I will bring again the shadow of the degrees, which is gone down in the sun dial of Ahaz, ten degrees backward. So the sun returned ten degrees, by which degrees it was gone down.
>
> Isaiah 38:7–8

> And this is the sign from the LORD to prove that he will do as he promised: I will cause the sun's shadow to move ten steps backward on the sundial of Ahaz!" So the shadow on the sundial moved backward ten steps.
>
> Isaiah 38:7–8 NLT

Can you believe this is in the Bible? The Lord is capable of anything!

Practical 10: Prep your car—or other daily space.

Place reminders for yourself in a place where you spend time every day. For me, that tends to be the car. For you, it may be an office, a kitchen, or a bedroom. I try to use every bit of time throughout my day to turn my heart to Him, but sometimes I get busy and forget. So I find ways to remind myself to constantly turn to Him, to open myself up to be with Him, to hear Him.

The best way for me to do that is to put sticky notes in various places in my car, usually the dashboard or steering wheel. My reminder notes don't usually contain Scripture passages; they're not the ones I use for memorizing or meditating on Scripture. (But you can use them any way you want!) These notes are literal reminders and contain only a few words. Sometimes I'll write, "Pray in tongues." Sometimes I'll just write, "Tongues." Or I'll say, "Worship in English. Worship in tongues."

I switch these out from week to week based on what I want to focus on.

Another thing I have done as a way to prep my car for focused times with Him is that I had my windows tinted really dark.

I like to worship Him any chance I get. And though I'm not ashamed or embarrassed, it *does* look a little strange to see someone driving beside you shouting or crying to "air." I thought it best to just tint my windows, so I could drive in peace while getting lost in Him.

Experience—His Presence in My Car

There have been times when He comes into my car like He does into my room. He has filled my car with His presence. Sometimes I just sense Him. I know He's there. I can feel Him, but it's all in the spiritual realm. Other times, though, He has shown Himself as a tangible dew. It's literally dew all over the inside of my car. I can feel it and even taste it. I call it "honeydew" because it's sweet. It's almost like honey!

One day, this dew came in, and I actually said, "Lord, this isn't possible. You don't come into a car like this." I rolled the windows down, and it was still there. I rolled them back up, and it was still there. Or, rather, *He* was still there! At first, it seemed crazy to me. But now, all I can do is laugh and just enjoy every minute I have with Him.

Practical 11: Focus on His name—or names.

In chapter 7, we talked about the importance of God's names. But I got a revelation of how powerful His name was when I gave my heart to Him and was saved. For me, He showed up as Salvation, as the Person of Salvation. Jesus's name means "God saves," so this would make sense. And then, when I went to Bible college, I gained a better understanding of His names. I learned that He has more names than just Jesus. On top of that, I realized that His names aren't merely identifiers like ours are. His names say who and what He is.

>He is the Bridegroom.
>
>He is Salvation.
>
>He is Healing.
>
>He is Faith.

His names aren't merely identifiers like ours are. His names say who and what He is.

So, here's what I want to share with you. When you are praying or worshiping, and He shows you a characteristic of

Himself, a certain aspect of His being, put a name to it. When you experience His peace, call Him Peace. When you experience happiness, call Him Joy. And then focus on that name. Whisper it, say it softly, over and over. Doing this helps me slow down and just bask in that side of Him. I believe it'll do the same for you. And I really believe He likes when I do it.

Practice His Presence

Now, I want you to try it. Think of a certain aspect of Him that means a lot to you or a side of Him that you've been wanting to learn more about. Put a name to that characteristic. Write it down. Meditate on it—for several days or weeks—but start today.

When I meditate on His name, I'll say it over and over, usually in a whisper. I say the name slowly and really drag it out. I say it, but I also hear myself saying it. It's amazing what this can do. Sometimes I'll sing His name to a worship song instead of singing that song's lyrics.

Don't forget Scripture. If He showed you a certain side of Him, you can bet there is a Scripture for it. Look it up! And study it out.

Experience—My Bridegroom Encounter

At one point, I went after the Lord as Bridegroom. I wanted to know what it was like to marry Him. When I married my wife, my eyes told me that she was standing by my side, and we went through a ceremony and a reception. I have vivid memories of that day. But with Jesus, it's just different. But I didn't know to what degree of "different" it was. So I told Him, "I want to *see* this. You're my Bridegroom, so what does it look like to marry You?"

I began to meditate on the name Bridegroom. I gave Him my vision and my mind, and I opened myself up for Him to show me what it looks like to be married to Him. I did this for several weeks, just like I suggested to you. And then, I saw Him.

I was driving my daughters to school, and I had just dropped off my youngest. As I turned into my older daughter's school—I guess the best way to explain it is that I kind of lost my vision for this world and gained *His* vision. I have heard this described as an open vision because I was still taking my daughter to school, but I was "seeing" His world.

Jesus was on one knee with a ring in His hand, and His hand was reaching for mine. I was standing, looking down at Him kneeling, and He was looking up at me and putting a ring on my finger!

I'm a guy. I have never been proposed *to*. But this moment was so real and so powerful! I truly saw Him as my Bridegroom!

Thank goodness I had my sunglasses on so my daughter didn't see me weeping. It was such an intense experience; I almost could not bear it. I dropped off my daughter and raced home to be alone with my Bridegroom!

Intimacy Activation Prayer

Pray your own words or use what I have here. But let's pray and put off the old mindset and put on the new.

Lord, open the eyes of my understanding about the secret place. Matthew 6:6 says to go into my closet and shut the door. What does that look like? What happens in the room where I am alone with You? How long do I stay? Show me what it's like. Give me new ideas and new ways to be alone with You. Teach me, oh Great Teacher!

Practice His Presence

Now, I want you to find out how He would want you to spend time with Him. Go to Him. But what we've discussed before Him and ask Him. As a reminder, here are the eleven practicals from this chapter:

- Practical 1: Find what works for you.
- Practical 2: Create an itinerary. Leave something blank.
- Practical 3: Set an expectation level each night.
- Practical 4: "Fast" time and ditch the itinerary.
- Practical 5: Use a devotional or a Bible promises book.

- Practical 6: Play a variety of music.
- Practical 7: Pray as Holy Spirit leads.
- Practical 8: Eat before you go in or eat with the Lord
- Practical 9: Accumulate the "practicals."
- Practical 10: Prep your car—or other daily space.
- Practical 11: Focus on His name—or names.

Don't make this difficult. You can simply say, "Lord, I have never whispered Your name like this." Or, "I don't usually sing in my prayer language. But I want to try it! I want to do that!"

And then just do it.

Chapter 10
Coming Away with Jesus
The Importance of Spending Time Alone with Him

*One thing have I asked of the Lord, **this will I earnestly seek**: that I should dwell in the house of the Lord all the days of my life, **that I should behold the fair beauty of the Lord**, and survey his temple. For in the day of mine afflictions he hid me in his tabernacle: **he sheltered me in the secret of his tabernacle**; he set me up on a rock.*

Psalm 27:4–5 Brenton

Throughout this book, I have used phrases like prayer closet, quiet time, and secret place. Because I have been living this intimate lifestyle with Jesus for several years, I sometimes forget what it was like when this "concept" was new to me. For someone unfamiliar with it, a prayer closet might sound confining, and "secret place" might sound mysterious. Recently, someone asked me how this secret place became real for *me*.

I had been around church and "church people" all my life. My grandpa was a preacher, and my parents were Christians and loved the Lord. But I had never heard of this kind of quiet place or prayer closet. And I certainly had never seen anything like this walked out.

When I had that face-to-face encounter with the Lord that I described at the beginning of this book, everything changed for me. I became so hungry for the word. I read and studied the Bible all day, and I listened to it on audio at night. I figured out I could read the New Testament in one weekend. And if I chose not to read, I could listen to the entire Bible in a weekend. Yet the hunger I had for the word and for Jesus felt impossible to satisfy.

I was reading books by people who were well-known for their teaching of the word and for moving in the gifts of the Spirit. I noticed there was one thing they all seemed to talk about—their alone time with the Lord. They all had different methods and experiences with their time alone with God, but they all seemed to talk about their prayer closet or secret place.

I still didn't completely understand a lot about this secret place, but I understood the word *prayer*, and I knew what a closet was, so I figured I could put the pieces together and try it for myself. So, one day I decided that I was going to work through the process of sitting before the Lord. I was going to get on my knees and just start there. So I did. I knelt down and started talking to God. After a few minutes, my knees started hurting. I grabbed a throw blanket, folded it up, and knelt on it. When that became uncomfortable, I got off my knees and sat on the blanket. Then I moved back into a kneeling position. Whatever I needed to do to keep my physical discomfort from driving me away from that quiet time, I did it. I shifted around and just kept praying and talking to Him. I asked Him to guide me through this process. I didn't even know what process I was asking Him to guide me through. I just knew that I was hungry for more of Him, and He was leading me to sit before Him, so He would show me what to do from there.

I did this off and on for months. Although I wanted to build up to staying there for an hour at a time, like the preachers I had been reading, I still hadn't reached it. But that was okay. I knew I was building, and my times with the Lord were so special that every minute became precious to me.

After those several months, my friend and I went to a conference in my hometown where a number of teachers and preachers were speaking. Like the books I had been reading, there seemed to be a common thread through all their messages. They spoke about intimacy with the Lord. They talked about spending quiet time with Him and what that looked like. And they talked about some of their experiences in those quiet places, things like dreams, visions, and encounters with the Lord.

During a time of worship at the conference, something happened to me. Probably the best way I can explain it is to say that a picture of the Lord was burned into the back of my eyelids. I saw a picture of Jesus, of His face. I saw Him so clearly and in such sharp focus that His face was all I could see every time I closed my eyes. And not just during that conference. That picture of His face was there, behind my eyelids, for weeks, months, actually.

The intimacy between Him and me had been building for those months before the conference, but I can tell you, it was like the fire—the love and infatuation I had for Him—was turned up ten times hotter. Now that I had Him in my eyesight constantly, all I wanted was to be alone with Him. All the time. But now, because of those books, the conference, and my practice times with Him, I knew what to do to satisfy my hunger for Him.

I want to be clear here: Satisfying the hunger doesn't mean the hunger stops. What satisfaction or fulfillment means to me is that I can get filled up during my alone times with Him, and then I can go about my day, work, and family life and know that He is always with me and He is continually drawing me back to Himself. And then, as soon as I have time to be with Him again, I can run back to my closet and get filled to overflowing. Again and again and again. It's a beautiful cycle.

I have learned so much during my alone times with Him, but one thing that has been made most real to me is the fact that He is always with me. I don't have to try to get to Him. He never left and never will. Absolutely never! Those times that I felt like He was far away, it was me. I was the one pulling back or withdrawing. Bible teacher and founder of Charis Bible College, Andrew Wommack, always says, "He's not the variable. He's the constant." Jesus is a constant and present reality for us. This is great news for us because if we ever feel withdrawn from Him, we don't have to work and work to "make God" come back to us. We simply turn our hearts to Him.

He is always with me. I don't have to try to get to Him. He never left and never will. Absolutely never!

Remember the satellite dish? Tuning into the Lord is simply a matter of turning our hearts. And this can be and should be a constant thing. It's both a possibility and a reality, and it's the only place to live from.

The Lord is calling us, His people, to see ourselves as who we are—His bride. We are the bride to the ultimate Bridegroom. But to fully walk in this, we must be intimate with Him. Not out of obligation, but out of infatuation.

I love how the New Living Translation talks about us, Jesus's bride:

> For I am jealous for you with the jealousy of God himself. I promised you as a pure bride to one husband—Christ.
>
> 2 Corinthians 11:2

> He did this to present her to himself as a glorious church without a spot or wrinkle or any other blemish. Instead, she will be holy and without fault.
>
> Ephesians 5:27

> Let us be glad and rejoice, and let us give honor to him. For the time has come for the wedding feast of the Lamb, and his bride has prepared herself.
>
> Revelation 19:7

> Then one of the seven angels who held the seven bowls containing the seven last plagues came and said to me, "Come with me! I will show you the bride, the wife of the Lamb."
>
> Revelation 21:9

Jesus isn't coming back for the rich or heroic. He's not coming back for those who have great faith and operate in miracles. He's coming back for His bride. A bride spends time alone with the bridegroom. A bride is intimate. A bride is a laid-down lover, seeking only her Groom.

That's who Jesus is looking for. That's who He is returning for.

He calls you by name.

He calls you His own.

He whispers to you,

"Come away. Let's be alone."

Additional Copyrights

Scripture quotations marked AMP are taken from the Amplified® Bible. Copyright © 2015 by The Lockman Foundation. Used by permission. www.lockman.org.

Scripture quotations marked AMPC were taken from the Amplified® Bible. Copyright © 1954, 1958, 1962, 1964, 1965, 1987 by The Lockman Foundation. Used by permission. www.lockman.org.

Scripture quotations marked Brenton are taken from the translation of the Greek Septuagint into English by Sir Lancelot Charles Lee Brenton. Published in 1851, and now in the Public Domain.

Scripture quotations marked CSB have been taken from the Christian Standard Bible®. Copyright © 2017 by Holman Bible Publishers. Used by permission. Christian Standard Bible® and CSB® are federally registered trademarks of Holman Bible Publishers.

Scripture quotations marked GNT are from the Good News Translation in Today's English Version, Second Edition. Copyright © 1992 by American Bible Society. Used by Permission.

Scripture quotations marked ICB have been taken from the Holy Bible, International Children's Bible®. Copyright© 1986, 1988, 1999, 2015 by Thomas Nelson. Used by permission.

Scripture quotations marked MEV have been taken from the Holy Bible, Modern English Version. Copyright © 2014 by Military Bible Association. Published and distributed by Charisma House. All rights reserved.

Scripture quotations marked NASB and NASB95 have been taken from the New American Standard Bible®. Copyright © 1960, 1971, 1977, 1995, 2020 by The Lockman Foundation. Used by permission. All rights reserved. www.lockman.org.

Scripture quotations marked NCV have been taken from the New Century Version®. Copyright © 2005 by Thomas Nelson. Used by permission. All rights reserved.

Scripture quotations marked NET have been taken from the New English Translation, NET Bible®. https://netbible.com. Copyright ©1996, 2019. Used with permission from Biblical Studies Press, L.L.C. All rights reserved.

Scripture quotations marked NIV have been taken from the Holy Bible, New International Version®, NIV®. Copyright © 1973, 1978, 1984, 2011 by Biblica, Inc.® Used by permission. All rights reserved worldwide.

Scripture quotations marked NKJV have been taken from the New King James Version®. Copyright © 1982 by Thomas Nelson. Used by permission. All rights reserved.

Scripture quotations marked NLT have been taken from the *Holy Bible*, New Living Translation. Copyright © 1996, 2004, 2015 by Tyndale House Foundation. Used by permission of Tyndale House Publishers, Inc., Carol Stream, Illinois 60188. All rights reserved.

Scripture quotations marked TLB have been taken from The Living Bible. Copyright © 1971 by Tyndale House Foundation. Used by permission of Tyndale House Publishers Inc., Carol Stream, Illinois 60188. All rights reserved.

Scripture quotations marked TPT are from The Passion Translation®. Copyright © 2017, 2018, 2020 by Passion & Fire Ministries, Inc. Used by permission. All rights reserved. ThePassionTranslation.com.

Scripture quotations marked VOICE are taken from The Voice™. Copyright © 2008 by Ecclesia Bible Society. Used by permission. All rights reserved.

Scripture quotations marked YLT have been taken from Young's Literal Translation. Public Domain.

Take your *message* and touch the *world*.

Made For More is a **Message Launch Program** with a mission to help people make a living doing what they are called to do, **one message launch at a time.**

MadeForMore.io features training to help you transform lives and communities with your calling, along with encouragement from Rigel and Jenna Drake-Garcia and the Made For More team. Receive guidance on how to write, publish and launch your God-given message, or sponsor a message you want to share, so you can **make a living doing what you are called to do.** You can check out our free training on how to write a marketable message for your ministry or sponsor a God-given message today at **MadeForMore.io**

You are made for *more!*
MadeForMore.io

Don't just survive your life. Thrive!

CRAVING JESUS

Discover your personal path to maintaining a long-lasting, fruitful relationship with Jesus.

I've come to know Jesus as a Person. Many people have been introduced to Christians, but not many have been introduced to Jesus. Whether you are thriving or surviving in life, I want to introduce you to the Person who saved the world, the King of kings, the Lord of lords, the One who holds the keys to victory, and the One who has captured my heart, fully and completely.

Author Kevin Lesh

In 2016, I had a radical encounter with God that changed my life. I fell in love with Jesus and set out on a journey to become more intimate with Him. I also wanted to share my practices with others. I realized just how many times someone inspired me to have an intimate relationship with the Lord but never showed me how. Well, I'm about to show you, so get ready!

This book won't only show you my personal experiences and reveal the impact of Scripture, worship, and prayer on my relationship with Jesus, but it will also become a practical guide for you so you, too, can know Jesus in your own intimate way. Discover your personal path to **enjoying your walk with the Father, and let Holy Spirit make Jesus real to you now, in this life.**

I was also led to write the follow-up of this book, *Intimate Encounters with King Jesus: A Guided Prayer Journal and Devotional Book to Help You Practice His Presence.* You can learn more about the prayer journal at **CravingJesus.tv.**

If you would like to partner with us and help others around the world to grow in intimacy with Jesus, you can learn more at **CravingJesus.tv/give, or simply scan the QR code below!**

Made in the USA
Columbia, SC
03 May 2023

15987935R00176